Soft drifts of Virginia bluebells and bright clumps of yellow and white daffodils create a charming spring picture in Louise Morse's Princeton, New Jersey, woodland garden.

EASY CARE
Shade Flowers

PATRICIA A. TAYLOR

A Fireside Book

PUBLISHED BY SIMON & SCHUSTER

New York London Toronto Sydney Tokyo Singapore

FIRESIDE

Simon & Schuster Building

Rockefeller Center

1230 Avenue of the Americas

New York, New York 10020

Copyright © 1993 by Patricia A. Taylor

Photos, except where indicated otherwise, by Patricia A. Taylor

Designed by Bonni Leon

Manufactured in the United States of America

10 9 8 7 6 5 4 3 2 1

Library of Congress Cataloging-in-Publication Data
Taylor, Patricia A.
  Easy care shade flowers / Patricia A. Taylor.
    p. cm.
  "A Fireside book."
  Includes bibliographical references and index.
  1. Shade-tolerant plants. 2. Gardening in the shade. 3. Low
    maintenance gardening.
    I. Title.
SB434.7.T39 1993
635.9'54–dc20   92-27901
                                                   CIP

ISBN: 0–671–75567–6

C O N T E N T S

SECTION THREE
The Plants 59

Section One

THE BASICS

Easy care shade flowers greet visitors to Bonnie Stafford's Princeton, New Jersey, home. Tucked into a bright shade border facing north and west, plants on the edge include long-blooming Luxuriant fringed bleeding heart, handsome clumps of bigroot geranium, and feathery plumes of Peach Blossom astilbe. The deep pink flowers in the middle are foxglove blossoms. Blue campanulas and, in the back, white goatsbeard complete this colorful garden picture.

Welcome to the color and beauty of shade gardening.

For too long, property owners have believed that only a few plants can grow in shade and, as a result, have filled darker areas of their grounds with monochromatic greenery or just a smattering of impatiens or begonias. Now, choosing from the easy care plants described in this book, you will soon find yourself looking from your windows and seeing colorful vistas of shade flowers from spring through fall and even, in warmer parts of the country, through winter as well.

Sounds good. But just what does "easy care" entail? The flowers in this book need to be given a proper home—that is, a setting that duplicates their natural habitat. For most plants, this means being placed in soil rich in organic matter, the kind of soil created when leaves drop to the forest floor and decay naturally. Once you place the plants in such good earth, you should have to do no further work aside from an occasional watering in times of drought.

Should your shade be caused by buildings rather than deciduous trees, you will have to step in for the absence of nature and add composted leaf mulch to your garden once a year.

These beautiful shade plants not only require little or no care but also can be grown in an environmentally responsible manner—which is, basically, the easiest way of all to nurture plants. Think of the thousands of flowers that thrive on their own in woodlands and shady dells across our country and around the world. These plants receive no extra attention in the way of fertilizers or pesticides. There's no reason why the flowers in your shade garden shouldn't be treated in the same carefree way. As an added bonus, all flowers in this book are propagated commercially, which means they do not have to be dug from the wild.

Before reading about the sumptuous and beautiful shade flowers described in this book and deciding which are right for your property, it is useful to know some simple shade gardening facts and design fundamentals.

Chapter One

INTRODUCTION TO
SHADE GARDENING

American columbine, here pictured in late April growing in a terrace wall in Bloomfield, Connecticut, exemplifies plants that need summer shade. Its beautiful red-and-yellow flowers bloom in spring sun and then its dark green foliage rests the remainder of the garden year in the coolness of shade formed by the leaves of nearby deciduous trees.

When my husband and I bought our house in 1975, I was dismayed at the sight of so many trees both on and bordering our small Princeton, New Jersey, property. The trees had all been planted in the late 1940s as new homeowners settled into the bare surroundings of one of Princeton's first housing developments. What happened on the two small streets of my neighborhood was the beginning of a grand-scale housing and planting pattern across the country.

I'm sure the first owners of our house, and of the homes abutting our property, found it hard to imagine that skinny, 6-foot-tall plants could grow into magnificent elms, oaks, sycamores, and maples. But grow these plantings did, crowding together and forming dense canopies of shade.

And I am sure that many of those buying heavily wooded properties today have much the same reaction that I did when we moved into our house. "I'll never be able to garden in such shade," I moaned. This book, filled with pictures and detailed descriptions of hundreds of easy care flowering plants, shows how very wrong I was.

It took a long time for me to become a shade gardening convert. Novice that I was, I firmly believed that you could not have lots of flowers without lots of sun. In order to get the gorgeous yellows, brilliant whites, luscious pinks, and cool blues to blossom in my beds, I led my husband on a sunlight quest. Five trees were cut down and quite a few others trimmed.

Presented with increased sunshine and more open space, I then began a search for plants, primarily easy care perennials because I was busy raising two daughters and working as a free-lance writer. Most flowers, whether as gifts or purchases, were plants that did best in sun or that could take four or five hours of shade at most. Several, however, were self-seeders so profligate that they seeded themselves in dark areas—and then went on to flower in them.

They taught me one of my first lessons: some plants, such as feverfew and European columbine, are so adaptable that they will bloom in shade as well as sun. Others, such as lamb's ears, were mistakenly planted in shaded spots (the sun was shining down at the time of planting) and looked quite handsome, though they did not flower as well as those in sunnier areas.

Thus, through trial, error, and luck, I began to learn about the shade tolerances of many plants. With each passing year it became more important for me to do so because though we had cut and trimmed our trees, our neighbors' trees were growing ever taller and their branches were extending ever wider. The battle for sunlight was becoming a losing one.

On the other hand, gardening in a shaded situation was becoming a pleasant occupation. Whenever I met another gardener, he or she would tell me about a plant that they either grew or that someone else had recommended for shade. Corinne Rowley of Hartford, Connecticut, introduced me to epimediums, wonderful dry shade plants with good-looking foliage and pretty spring flowers. Eleanor Taylor, my mother-in-law, gave me the blue-flowered American Jacob's ladder and fringed bleeding heart, which is covered with pink blossoms in spring.

At the same time, nursery catalogue offerings of shade plants began to expand with the greening of American properties. I bought the Lenten rose, so named because its violet-tinged pale green blossoms start their three-month bloom period shortly after Lent begins, and the yellow corydalis, which flowers in bright shade from May to September.

Shade gardening, I was beginning to appreciate, is very colorful gardening. It is also elegant gardening. Shade plants beguile viewers not only with their flowers but also with their luxurious foliage. In a shade garden, one is not only a painter but a sculptor as well, working with voluptuous leaf forms and delicate foliages.

There's another aspect of shade gardening that I have come to appreciate. By its very nature, it is a restricted, cozy sort of gardening. Though a garden can extend over acres, each segment of a shade garden is a relatively compact, individual unit. A shade garden is a manageable garden.

We have now lived in our house for almost twenty years. While I still grow many sun plants, I have fallen in love with the tranquil beauty and grace of my shade gardens. Meanwhile, new neighbors have moved next door and one of the first things they did was to cut down a huge maple tree bordering my property. "You will have lots of sun to grow plants now," they told me. I, the person who was once adamant about cutting down trees, am sure they will be unable to understand why my husband and I are currently reviewing different flowering trees to see what will best keep the sun away from our wonderful collection of beautiful, easy care shade plants.

UNDERSTANDING THE NATURE OF SHADE

To me, one of the most frustrating aspects of growing plants in less than full sun has been and remains the difficulty in pinpointing the seasonality of shade. Just think about it: there is not one single open spot on the North American continent that receives the same amount of light each day.

And not only does shade vary by season, it also changes by time of day. There is nothing extraordinary about noting that an area soaking up morning sun can be in dense shade by noon; yet, for some reason, it is difficult for me to remember this when I am planting a flower in the morning. I look at the sunny spot and

think, "That's perfect." And it's usually not until several days later, when I'm on an afternoon inspection tour, that I'll realize what a mistake I have made in placing a sun lover in such a dark area.

And though it may not seem so to the gardener, morning and afternoon sun are very different to the plant. In general, morning sun is cool sun and preferred by moisture-loving plants. Early afternoon sun hits plants at the hottest time of the day, when they might already be tired and thirsty from high summer temperatures. Few shade plants tolerate early afternoon sun but many sun plants can take morning shade.

KINDS OF SHADE

Throughout this book, I will make reference to the suitability of plants for different kinds of shade. Though most of these plants should do well in several different shade settings, it might be helpful to define just what the different terms mean.

Dappled Shade. This is the kind of shade spotted with sunlight and is possible only in a woodland setting. The dapples—or sun spots—change with the movement of the sun across the sky. For purposes of this book, dappled shade refers to areas where sun spots manage to touch directly upon a plant's foliage for at least an hour.

Bright Shade. This is used to describe settings without direct sun but which are brightly lit. In general, the locations behind white, north-facing building walls fit such descriptions as well as the open areas at the edge of woodlands.

High Shade. Only possible in a wooded setting, this is the shade that results when the lower limbs of a tree are cut. Think of how much brighter a high-ceilinged room is than a low-ceilinged room.

In a bright shade setting, fringed bleeding heart (left), bishop's cap (above), and yellow corydalis bloom away. Though direct sun does not reach these plants, they can still thrive in the ample light reflected from the white aluminum siding.

Heavy or Dense Shade. This is the kind of light found in an enclosed spot, one in which there are no bright materials for light to reflect from. Dark buildings surrounding a small plot can cause heavy shade. Heavily branched trees can block out sun from above and, with limbs almost touching the ground, can also screen out side light. Very few plants grow in settings that are densely shaded for the entire day.

Part Shade. Most plants grow in part shade; that is, in areas receiving sun some of the day and shade the remainder. How much sun and how much shade is, of course, crucial. In this book, no more than five hours of direct sun constitutes partial shade.

Summer Shade. This refers to areas that receive lots of winter sun and little if any summer sun. The ground under deciduous trees is

a good example. In addition, the sun is so low in winter that its rays can creep under fir trees that cover the ground with dense shade in the summer. Many early-blooming bulbs and perennials, such as winter aconites and pheasant's-eyes, have evolved to thrive in such situations.

RECOGNIZING THE DRAWBACKS OF SHADE

Despite my increasing appreciation for shade gardening, I readily admit that it has its negative aspects. The first has to do with the buildings and trees causing the shade.

Buildings store heat during the summer day and then release much of it in the evening. Plants in shade gardens next to buildings often need to be tolerant of heat and will require extra water. Care should be taken, however, that plants are not placed near downspouts, which can drown a garden in heavy rainstorms.

Tree roots not only crowd out other plants but also compete for soil nutrients and water. In my experience, maples, beeches, sycamores, and black locusts are the worst. Their shallow roots will spread up to 50 feet away from their home base. I am constantly digging into, and then having to cut or hack away at, tree roots running rampant under my garden beds. At such moments, I long for the joys of a garden far from trees, a place where one can dig easily into the soil without constantly hitting obstacles.

GARDEN PESTS

Pests are part of nature's balancing act and are endemic to all gardens. Those that are especially prone to creating havoc in shaded areas are black vine weevils, deer, slugs, and their close relatives, snails.

While not restricted to shade gardens, black vine weevils prefer to munch on shade-thriving plants, particularly those in the rhododendron, euonymus, hedera, and vinca genera.

Gardens shaded by buildings have to cope with heat absorbed throughout the day. The gorgeous easy care shade flowers thriving by Liz Fillo's garage in Princeton, New Jersey, seem to be unaware that the thermometer on the wall above them registered over 100°F when this photograph was taken on July 18 (the official high for the day was in the low 90s). The flowers are Gruss un Aachen roses, a tangle of Graham Thomas woodbine and goldflame honeysuckles, and the annual Madagascar periwinkle.

Often called taxus weevils, they count among their favorites plants belonging to the Taxus genus, commonly known as yews.

You know black vine weevils are at work when you see little notches all over the leaf edges of your plants. These notches are caused by the adults, who come out at night to disfigure your garden dreams. During the day, these black, long-snouted creatures nestle in leaf litter and cool, moist soil—the kind of condition existing in most shade gardens.

In the course of time—usually after a three-week feast—the females lay eggs, and that's when the tempo of destructive damage increases significantly. The eggs hatch into grubs, which burrow their way into the soil and eat the roots of whatever plant happens to be within striking distance. This root damage is more deadly to the overall health of a plant than the leaf notching.

To date, there is no known black vine weevil antidote that will totally eradicate the insect without destroying the plants that it feeds on. Many gardeners fight this pest by drenching the soil with chemical poisons to kill the grubs and by spraying the foliage several times to kill the adults. Using lethal chemicals, this regime merely reduces temporarily the black vine wee-

vil population! These are tough critters.

It appears, however, that so much work is not necessary. Research by Jim Hanula of the University of Connecticut demonstrates that a *single* application of a foliage spray in mid-July—which is about five weeks after the adults have emerged and started chewing on leaves—can reduce black vine weevils to acceptable levels (plants do not die but some foliage disfigurement occurs).

To people like me, even a single application of a lethal chemical poison is too much. Research on pesticide alternatives is being conducted, and it appears that several parasitic nematodes have the potential for reducing black vine weevil populations. Since these predators are not yet commercially available, I rely on a trial approach to see what works and what does not as far as black vine weevil damage is concerned. As shown in the box, there are quite a few shade

SELECTED SHADE FLOWERS RESISTANT TO BLACK VINE WEEVILS

In my gardens, black vine weevils avoid the following:

Flowering Onions (*Alliums*)
Late winter and early spring bulbs
Cuckoo Flower (*Cardamine pratensis*)
Chinese Bleeding Heart (*Dicentra spectabilis*)
Yellow Archangel (*Galeobdolon luteum*)
Lenten Rose (*Helleborus orientalis*)
Variegated Hosta (*H. undulata*)

Candytuft (*Iberis sempervirens*)
Impatiens (*I. wallerana*)
Christmas Fern (*Polystichum acrostichoides*)
Flowering Raspberry (*Rubus odoratus*)
Feverfew (*Tanacetum parthenium*)
Periwinkle (*Vinca minor*)

plants that these pests leave alone on my property.

Deer are a garden predator of increasing concern throughout the country. Since they traditionally make their homes in wooded settings, they are particularly associated with shade gardens. Though there are plants that deer do not prefer (see the listing below), in the final analysis a deer will eat anything if it is hungry enough. And with the almost exponential increase in deer populations in suburban areas across the country, there are a lot of hungry deer roaming through backyards and front lawns. No matter what you may read about repellents in the forms of soaps, sprays, powders, scarecrows, or human hairballs, the only truly effective deer deterrent is a high fence.

Slugs and snails are endemic to shade gardens. Because of their aversion to hot, dry conditions, they can only exist in cool, moist places. Since a slug is basically a defrocked snail, control methods for the one also apply to the other.

Though it is hard to remain rational about these creatures as they devour one beautiful flower after another, it might help to remember that they perform a beneficial recycling function in eating vegetable matter. Along with fungi and bacteria, they are aids in the composting process. Slugs are ubiquitous in all areas outside of desert conditions. In the final analysis, every gardener has to learn to coexist with them.

The concept of using beer traps as a control method is useless. In a myth-breaking yet totally ignored article published about twenty years ago in *Farmstead* magazine, Dr. Steve Katona wrote that slugs are attracted to the yeast in beer. He demonstrated that a mixture of dry yeast and water will attract more slugs than plain beer. The beer is more lethal, he explained, because the slugs become intoxicated in it, lose their bearings, and drown. The problem, as many gardeners have discovered, is that more slugs are attracted to the area where the beer is placed than are actually killed in the beer.

It is better by far, I have found over the years, to create a hostile environment for the slugs as well as to grow plants that they do not like. For instance, slugs do not like the bitter taste of tannin in wood. A gardener who sprinkles a 4-inch-to-6-inch-wide path of fresh wood chips (redwood chips are particularly effective in foiling California snails) around the edge of a garden should find few slugs crossing the barrier. While diatomaceous earth (the prickly, fossilized remains of tiny sea creatures) also makes an effective slug barrier, it can cause problems if particles are inhaled by gardeners.

Research by scientists at Princeton University and Bell Laboratories has demonstrated that slugs have definite likes and dislikes when

SELECTED SHADE FLOWERS RESISTANT TO DEER

Given a choice, deer will not eat the following:

Common Monkshood (*Aconitum napellus*)
Flowering Onions (*Alliums*)
Foxglove (*Digitalis purpurea*)

Daffodils (*Narcissus*)
Lamb's Ears (*Stachys byzantina*)
Feverfew (*Tanacetum parthenium*)

it comes to dining. They will not only stay away from the tannin in wood but from a large number of plants as well. Shade plants that slugs leave alone in my garden are listed in the box.

USING THIS BOOK TO CREATE A SHADE GARDEN

It is easy and fun to create your own shade garden. In the next chapter I present some basic design pointers and then show how I used these in planting a small shade garden at the side of my house.

Section II contains profiles of eight gardens. Scattered across the country, these demonstrate both the diversity of interests in creating a garden and the astonishing range of plants and combinations possible in a shade garden setting. In every case, a list of recommended easy care shade flowers is provided. If you have any question about the proper identification of a popularly named plant, check the plant index in the back of the book.

Section III presents detailed discussions of shade plants for gardens: shrubs; groundcovers and wall climbers; bulbs; annuals and biennials; astilbes, ferns, and hostas; and perennials. There are over 350 plants discussed—all of them not only wonderful shade flowers but also capable of growing in gardens throughout our nation. Plants such as camellias, which can only be grown in limited geographical ranges, are not covered in this book. Using the mail-order nursery sources at the end of each chapter you will

SELECTED SHADE FLOWERS RESISTANT TO SLUGS

In my garden, slugs avoid the following:

Hardy Begonia (*B. grandis*)
Wax Begonia (*B. semperflorens—cultorum* hybrids)
Late winter bulbs
Cuckoo Flower (*Cardamine pratensis*)
Fringed Bleeding Heart (*Dicentra eximia*)
Chinese Bleeding Heart (*Dicentra spectabilis*)
Foxglove (*Digitalis purpurea*)
Yellow Archangel (*Galeobdolon luteum*)

Lenten Rose (*Helleborus orientalis*)
Candytuft (*Iberis sempervirens*)
Impatiens (*I. wallerana*)
Sensitive Fern (*Onoclea sensibilis*)
American Jacob's Ladder (*Polemonium reptans*)
Christmas Fern (*Polystichum acrostichoides*)
Gold Moss (*Sedum acre*)
Shrubs
Feverfew (*Tanacetum parthenium*)

be able to obtain any plant you choose. Names and addresses for all firms are given at the back of the book.

Finally, I would like to make clear that this is not an encyclopedic discussion of shade gardening. For those who would like to delve further into the beauties of this subject, I have provided recommended readings throughout. Two basic shade gardening books that are appropriately mentioned here, and that are referred to often, are *Gardening in the Shade* by Harriet K. Morse and *The Complete Shade Gardener* by George Schenk.

Frederick and Mary Ann McGourty practice their nationally acclaimed design skills at Hillside Gardens Nursery in Norfolk, Connecticut. This section of their garden, photographed on July 1, illustrates both high and dappled shade. Perennials in the border, from left to right, include lady's mantle, silvermound artemisia (A. schmidtiana), and Peach Blossom astilbe. A magnificent climbing hydrangea spirals up the ash tree on the right.

Chapter Two

DESIGNING A
SHADE GARDEN

Courtesy of *Fine Gardening* magazine

White-flowered honesty, pink foxgloves, multicolored caladiums, and yellow pansies (Viola 'Golden Champion') all flourish in late spring in the Atlanta, Georgia, garden of landscape architect William T. Smith. These plants survive Georgia's brutal heat, Smith feels, primarily because he has placed them in carefully prepared soil.

I believe that when creating a shade garden—or any garden for that matter—people should do what pleases them most. And one of the best ways to learn just what is pleasing is to experiment with different plants and different combinations.

There is no set formula to follow. What works for one person or culture, for example, might not be perfect for another. Think of the beauty inherent in a sparse, carefully sculpted Japanese rock garden and in a chaotic, colorful English cottage garden. Though totally different, each has a special appeal.

While there are no hard-and-fast rules as to what constitutes good garden design, there are several basic questions you need to review when starting a shade garden. These include the reasons for your garden, the amount of light it will receive, and the kinds of flowers you wish to include.

centrate the flowering period into one short season (say the month you vacation in your country home)? Information on blooming period is provided for each plant described in Section III.

3 Do you want to experiment with many different plants or do you want to install a garden and then forget about any further plant additions? Both kinds of gardens, as shown in the profiles in Section II, are possible for easy care gardeners.

Considering these options will narrow your plant choices. Neither impatiens nor yellow corydalis, for example, are good cut flowers but they are both long-blooming decorative border plants. Though not flowering as long as these two, the native fringed bleeding heart looks handsome in gardens outdoors as well as in vases indoors. The function you assign your garden will determine which of these plants is best for you.

PINPOINTING THE GARDEN'S FUNCTION

The purpose you assign a garden determines its form. In reading this book, you have already made one key decision: the garden will be a low-maintenance one. That is, your garden will be filled with plants that need little care other than a weekly watering. Indeed, many of the flowers in this book grow on their own in woods with only the rainfall that nature provides.

Other questions that need to be reviewed are:

1 Do you want a garden to look at or do you want one that will supply you with cut flowers? Perhaps you want both. The individual plant descriptions in Section III of this book make note of flowers that are particularly striking in indoor arrangements.

2 Do you want something in bloom throughout the growing year or do you want to con-

ASSESSING THE KIND OF SHADE

This is one of the most important considerations in planning a shade garden. As mentioned in Chapter 1, shade varies, and plants react differently to each variation. A bright shade situation with two hours of direct morning sun, for example, is quite different from a setting that receives heavy shade most of the day and four hours of direct sun in the afternoon.

Often, you have to learn by trial and error what plants will work. As shown in the picture, I planted a row of three Rocket ligularias in a small, brightly shaded border. They were all given well-drained, humus-rich soil and located close to a hose so that they could easily be watered in early morning or late afternoon. The growing conditions were uniform and, I thought, perfect. The ligularias were planted about 40 inches apart at a time of day when the border inches high and spikes that soared to 37 inches.

Since the picture was taken, the bottom two plants have been removed from the border. Hostas (*H. plantaginea* and *H. ventricosa*), flowering raspberry, fernleaf corydalis, and chelones (*C. glabra* and *C. lyonii*) all flower quite well in their place. The cedar tree, which is on my neighbor's property, continues to grow, albeit slowly. In time, I shall probably have to transplant the last of the ligularias in this border.

The moral of this story is that the kind and amount of shade your garden site receives is a crucial consideration in determining the kinds of plants to grow. Information on shade requirements is presented with the plant descriptions in Section III.

REVIEWING THE HARDINESS ZONE

Plants react to temperatures as well as light. All the planning in the world will go for naught if a plant is not capable of growing in your climate area. One crucial factor, generally referred to as a plant's hardiness, describes the degree of winter cold a plant can tolerate. The U.S. Department of Agriculture uses the concept of climate zones to describe hardiness. Winter temperatures (that is, average low readings) assigned by the USDA to each zone are:

Zone 1	below −50°
Zone 2	−50° to −40°
Zone 3	−40° to −30°
Zone 4	−30° to −20°
Zone 5	−20° to −10°
Zone 6	−10° to 0°
Zone 7	0° to 10°
Zone 8	10° to 20°
Zone 9	20° to 30°
Zone 10	30° to 40°

Some plants are quite persnickety about the shade settings in which they will flower. Growing conditions for the 5 Rocket ligularias pictured here were uniform — with the exception of direct sunlight. The plant at the bottom received only ½ hour of full sun; the plant at the top, 5 hours.

was in bright shade.

Though I knew that sunlight did touch down upon the border, I had not taken into account the shade pattern created by a nearby red cedar. The plant at the bottom of the picture received only half an hour of direct sun and the ligularia at the top almost three hours.

The addition of about two and a half hours of direct sun made a striking difference in plant performance. The one receiving the least sun had a foliage clump reaching 13 inches in height and flower spikes reaching 22 inches. The one receiving almost three hours not only had many more flowers but also foliage which grew 27

POOR SOIL SHADE FLOWERS

Goutweed (*Aegopodium podagraria* 'Variegatum')
Bugleweed (*Ajuga reptans*)
European Columbine (*Aquilegia vulgaris*)
White Wood Aster (*Aster divaricatus*)
Fernleaf Corydalis (*C. cheilanthifolia*)
Spanish Squill (*Endymion hispanicus*)
Epimedium (*Epimedium*)
Yellow Archangel (*Galeobdolon luteum*)
Tawny Daylily (*Hemerocallis fulva*)
Lance Leaf Hosta (*H. lancifolia*)
Variegated Hosta (*H. undulata*)
Blue Hosta (*H. ventricosa*)

Yellow Flag Iris (*I. pseudacorus*)
Big Blue Lobelia (*L. siphilitica*)
'Ice Follies' Daffodil (*Narcissus*)
Sensitive Fern (*Onoclea sensibilis*)
Chinese Basil (*Perilla frutescens*)
Old Garden Phlox (*P. paniculata*)
Lungwort (*Pulmonaria saccharata*)
Flowering Raspberry (*Rubus odoratus*)
Siberian Squill (*Scilla siberica*)
Feverfew (*Tanacetum parthenium*)
Spiderwort (*Tradescantia x andersoniana*)
Periwinkle (*Vinca minor*)

The zone information accompanying each plant description in Section III refers to these temperatures. The great majority of shade flowers described in this book are suitable for zones 4–8, and zone 9 on the West Coast.

EVALUATING THE GARDEN FLOOR

This is crucial in terms of both design and plant choice. There are four key factors that must be reviewed:
1 What kind of soil is in your garden floor?
2 Is the ground dry or wet?
3 Are there tree roots in the proposed garden area?
4 Is the floor attractive?

KIND OF SOIL

Most shade flowering plants evolved in woodland situations. As such, they require soil rich in organic matter, the kind created by falling leaves and dying vegetation.

There are, then, few shade garden sites that can be planted without prior soil preparation. This is basically at odds with my credo of no maintenance. Those gardeners who do not wish to take the time to evaluate their soil and who want to simply stick some plants in the ground and let them flower at will should check the plants listed above. All are tough shade flowers that I grow, most in clay soil pockmarked with shallow roots from shrubs or trees. Be warned that the groundcovers will become invasive if placed in humus-rich soil.

Those wishing to enjoy the full diversity of beautiful shade plants might take as a motto the old saying, "A stitch in time saves nine." The "stitch" in this case is proper soil preparation. After that, all you have to do is choose plants appearing in this book, add leaf mulch or organic matter once a year, water weekly (more or less, depending on the plant), and then sit back and watch these beautiful flowers perform for you just as they do in their ancestral woodlands.

William T. Smith, a member of the American Society of Landscape Architects (ASLA), is an ardent advocate of proper soil preparation. He's also the kind of person who practices what he preaches. The picture on page 19 is of a shady corner in his Atlanta, Georgia, garden. Included are flowers such as foxgloves, honesty, and pansies—plants that thrive in his specially prepared soil. Smith feels that all annuals, biennials, and perennials should be given a proper home in which to flourish.

As he recommends for his clients, Smith excavated his garden soil to a depth of 18 inches (Georgia's red clay is fine for most trees and shrubs, he says, but is rough on perennials). Next he installed a drainage pipe, since clay is notorious for its water-retaining properties; the roots of many plants will rot away in such soil. He then refilled his garden area with a mixture of topsoil, rotted manure, sand, ground-bark mulch, lime, and perlite. The result, as pictured on page 19, is a handsome collection of flowers that can be grown in Georgia's gardens.

At beautiful Hillside Gardens Nursery in Norfolk, Connecticut, Frederick and Mary Ann McGourty exhibit superb flower and foliage combinations in shaded settings. Here, the chartreuse green in the frothy blossoms of lady's mantle is echoed in the edging on the Hosta fortunei *'Aureo-marginata'.*

DRYNESS OF AREA

Easy care gardeners do not want to water every day nor do they wish to pull out plants rotting in bog situations. To eliminate such chores, sur-

vey the dryness of the area in which you are about to plant.

Soil near a rainpipe on the north side of a building is usually constantly moist; I've placed yellow flag irises in such a situation and they thrive. Soil under shrubs with spreading roots and suckers tends to dry out quickly; I've planted white wood asters in such an area and they bloom away with abandon. Had I reversed the plantings, neither flower would have done well.

Individual plant descriptions in Section III often include information on whether a plant favors a dry or a wet setting. In addition, the two California arboretums contributing plant recommendations (see pages 60 and 61) listed only flowers suitable for dry shade.

PRESENCE OF TREE ROOTS

As mentioned in Chapter 1, many tree roots are major competitors for soil nutrients and moisture. You know you have a tree-root problem if you try to plant a flower and can't dig down more than two inches.

While it is possible to build up soil above a tree's roots (see picture on page 98 for a very successful example), really obnoxious roots will climb right into the new garden setting. In such situations, shallow-rooted plants (most groundcovers fit into this category) and small bulbs are best. Epimediums also thrive among tree roots.

ATTRACTIVENESS OF FLOOR

Once you've picked out the area where you will be placing your plants, step back and take a look at the total setting. Often grass has a hard time growing in dark corners. Will your flowers and shrubs surround a rather barren lawn setting? On the other hand, will brambles and wild honeysuckle make a mess of a woodland garden?

In the first case, you might want to consider covering the open ground with bricks, bluestone, or gravel. In the second, you might want to clear the weeds and install groundcovers such as Allegheny foamflower, yellow archangel, or creeping phlox.

CHECKING OUT THE GARDEN WALLS

By their very nature, all shade gardens have walls—that is, trees or buildings that block sunlight. If the "walls" were banished, the shade in the garden would cease to exist. These walls, then, are crucial to the design of your garden. There are several questions to consider when incorporating walls into your garden scheme.

1 Do you want the walls covered? With regard to buildings, trellises can be affixed to their sides, and vines such as clematis and hardy fuchsia can ramble up on them. Or shrubs can be placed next to a building wall and these can form a backdrop to the garden bed. Even tree trunks can be cloaked, as Frederick and Mary Ann McGourty so beautifully demonstrate with a climbing hydrangea at their Hillside Gardens Nursery in Norfolk, Connecticut (see picture on page 18).

2 Are the walls attractive in their own right? As shown on the right, Liz Fillo created an exquisite shade garden featuring the sculptural form of a dogwood tree. Gay Bumgarner, as described on pages 44–47, cut a path through her woods and walled her garden by using trees as triumphal arches.

3 Do you want to add more walls? Often the wall is free-standing—a lone tree or a blank side of a house—and needs to be somehow connected with the garden. Fences or brick walls can often unite the setting and make it appear more attractive. Shrubbery, in the form of hedges, can also be used to create a wall in a shaded setting.

CONSIDERING THE FOLIAGE EFFECT

Shade gardeners almost have an embarrassment of riches with which to work—not only exquisitely beautiful flowers but also sumptuous foliage in many variegated patterns and hues. Indeed, some shade gardeners prefer to have only a minimum number of flowering plants and to concentrate on leaf patterns and textures.

Outstanding examples of beautiful foliage-and-flower combinations can be seen at Hillside Gardens Nursery in Norfolk, Connecticut. Visitors to the Nursery may stroll through the adjacent private gardens; many of the plants in these gardens are for sale at the shop. One of my favorite combinations, pictured on page 23, shows the chartreuse green of the lady's mantle picked up by the yellow-green edging on the *Hosta fortunei* 'Aureo-marginata'.

In one of my borders, pictured on page 79, I played with different colored greens—the warmer greens of the flowering raspberry and the August lily flanking the dark green of the *Hosta ventricosa*. While this little plant three-some has something blooming from July through August, the flowers do not always

stand out; the foliage pattern helps to give it continued interest.

If you feel overwhelmed with detail in beginning a garden, don't worry about foliage at first. As you become familiar with different plants, you will soon see combinations to try.

THINKING SMALL

All plants come with a price: if not in dollars, then in time spent planting and maintaining them. And no matter how highly recommended the shade plants in this book are, there will

"Simple elegance" is an apt phrase to describe Liz Fillo's design scheme for a shady area on her Princeton, New Jersey, property. With the graceful limbs of a native dogwood as the structural centerpiece, this garden spot has year-round interest. In spring, the woodruff groundcover is blanketed with star-white flowers. Multicolored caladiums are attractive from June to frost. In July, when this photograph was taken, yellow spikes of Rocket ligularia burst forth. Three weeks later, in early August, the white flowers of Royal Standard hostas begin to bloom.

always be one that looks absolutely smashing everywhere in the world except in your garden. Thus, the last design fundamental for novices is to start small.

Granted, it is hard to limit your choice when there are hundreds of tempting plants in this book. Nevertheless, do so. Pick no more than three or four plants by season of bloom (say, late winter, early spring, spring, summer, and fall) and then group them as you please in a manageable border.

Since all plants in this book are easy care, you will have lots of color and instant success the first year. Some plants, however, will do better than others, while one or two may be either a disaster or just not up to par. Discard these, perhaps enlarge the border or start a new one, and then add several more plants the following year. Stop the process whenever you like.

A CASE HISTORY: THE AUTHOR'S GARDEN

While it's fine to read about principles in the abstract, it's not always easy to translate them into concrete practices. Here's how I used the above guidelines to create a small shaded garden by one side of my house.

This part of our property had always been rather dark and unattractive. When workmen finished putting an addition on our house in 1987, it was a disaster. Our heavy clay soil had been firmly packed down by both machines and workers, and the new wing left just a narrow 9-foot-wide strip of land between the house and an old lilac bush.

When we pruned the lilac, we were left with a foliage arch over the area. With this airy ceiling and a walled corner formed by our original house and the new addition, we realized we had the beginnings of a "garden room"—an enclosed, defined space filled with plants.

The lilac bush on one side and the house on the other needed to be joined together to form an entire unit. My husband did this by building a 3-foot-high lattice fence. One part of the fence skirts the property border, behind the lilac. The second blocks the rear of the garden and comes equipped with a gate leading into the backyard. We left the front entrance to this garden unfenced, as an invitation to guests to go through it into the backyard.

BEFORE. Though never attractive, this narrow side strip appeared as a wasteland when workmen finished putting an addition on the house.

We now had a defined area measuring 9 feet by 9.5 feet. With the walls taken care of, we turned our attention to the "floor." It was wretched. Since we knew it would be next to impossible to grow grass in the area, we made a path of dry-laid brick through the garden. This not only simplified upkeep but also contributed a touch of color, as the dull red of the old brick contrasts nicely with the surrounding plants throughout the year.

The brick path split the garden area into two borders, one surrounding the lilac bush and the other next to the house. To add interest to the latter, we created a small raised bed in one corner. This little bed is edged with a 6-inch-high arc of vertical bricks.

All the soil in this part of the garden was just about unusable as far as growing plants goes. Fortunately, we had a well-rotted pile of horse manure—the result of a perennials-for-manure barter with one of the carpenters who worked on the addition. To this we added bags of sand and peat moss, and dug the mixture in to a depth of at least 2 feet.

Because of the root system of the lilac, it was not possible to improve this soil to any great degree. Fortunately, some tough shade plants were already growing in this area. I cleaned out many of the sensitive ferns, told the ajuga to stay at the very front of the border, and pared back the variegated hosta to just one small clump.

In front of this border, I planted short perennials with dramatically contrasting foliages, plants such as the fernleaf corydalis, bugloss, cuckoo flower, bloodroot, pink foamflower, and Japanese painted fern. Taller plants, such as a flowering raspberry bush and wood asters, filled up the back.

On the house side of the garden, in a narrow border only 18 inches deep, I planted bloodroots, astilbes, American Jacob's ladders, a variegated hosta, and lungworts. This section of the garden joins the area in front of the raised arc. Here I put fringed bleeding heart and yellow corydalis, two closely related plants with lovely blue-green foliage. Even more important, from a color point of view, is that the bleeding heart spouts pink flowers for at least three months, starting in early May, and the bright

AFTER. With the existing lilac bush as a leafy archway, a red brick path and a lattice fence were built as additional structural elements. Flowers blooming in the right border, from bottom to top, are blue American Jacob's ladders, blue lungworts, and pink fringed bleeding hearts.

yellow flowers of the corydalis are in bloom from late May to September (see picture on page 14).

A 'Blue Umbrellas' hosta was originally placed in the little raised bed above these two plants. Unfortunately it outgrew its assigned quarters after two years and has since been replaced by a hardy begonia. This last has proven particularly successful because of its late-season bloom. It is flanked on both sides by red epimediums whose red-tinged foliage looks lovely with that of the begonia.

Thus, using the guidelines reviewed earlier, it was easy to create a quite colorful garden. We took into account the soil (enriching it where we could and making do where we couldn't), the walls or structures enclosing the garden, and foliage contrasts.

Flower bloom in the garden starts in April with brilliant white bloodroots, blue and pink lungworts, and yellow fernleaf corydalis. In May, this garden is at its peak with the continued bloom of the lungworts plus the blue American Jacob's ladders and pink bleeding hearts in one border (see picture on page 27) and blue bugloss, pink cuckoo flower, and pink foamflower in the other.

The focus of attention in the garden bounces back and forth between the borders. In June, for example, the white plumes of the astilbe appear at the end of the house border, and the first deep pink blossoms of the flowering raspberry open across the way. In July, the light blue flowers of the variegated hosta join these last, plus the continued bloom of the fringed bleeding heart and the yellow corydalis.

Foliage color contributes a refreshing accent to the garden picture during the hot, tired month of August. The variegated hosta adds white, the lungwort splashes of silver gray, and the Japanese painted fern a tinge of maroon on the mid-ribs of its ghostly, greenish-white leaves. Cool September breezes welcome two new flowers to the border: white wood asters and pink hardy begonias.

From April through September flowers are blooming in this little shaded spot. And my only contribution to this scene, after the initial planting, has been a weekly watering in times of drought and a dressing of leaf mulch in spring. The flowers are all easy care plants that grow without pesticides or extra fertilizers. In addition, they are all packed in so tightly that there simply isn't room for weeds.

This garden is my little gem and I love it. Following the very basic precepts I have presented in this chapter, and using the wonderful plants described in this book, you too can have many shade gems of your own.

Section Two
THE GARDENS

Lavender and white Japanese anemones, red nasturiums, and yellow and pink tuberous begonias brighten up an October shade garden at The Old Milano Hotel in Gualala, California.

To me, one of the marvelous aspects of gardening is that no two creations are alike. Even neighbors back-to-back will have different plant combinations and settings.

And not only are gardens varied but so too are the reasons for gardening. Some gardeners grow flowers for esthetic purposes while others are avowed conservationists, and still others just like to look out a window and see something pretty.

This section illustrates the diversity of shade gardening—including the plants, the settings, and the goals—by profiling eight different gardens. Four of these are special-interest gardens open to the public. The others are private gardens, each serving different purposes.

In every profile, however, the gardener or organization has provided a list of favorite easy care shade flowers. A brief description accompanies each plant; the first designation (shrub, bulb, annual, etc.) refers to the chapter in Section III that contains more detailed information about the plant. Whether your shade garden is in the city or the woods, on the seashore or a riverbank, there is an easy care plant here that suits your own unique approach to gardening.

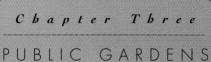

Chapter Three

PUBLIC GARDENS

Visits to other gardens are not only visual but also educational experiences. This beautiful red-flow-ered plumleaf azalea, for example, was photographed on August 30 at Garden in the Woods in Framingham, Massachusetts. Most horticultural literature insists that this shrub blooms in July and is not hardy north of Washington, D.C.!

Shade gardening is immeasurably enriched by the existence of small, special-interest public gardens. These institutions act as environmental custodians, serving as horticultural savings banks that not only artistically display beautiful plants but also commercially propagate them so that they will not have to be depleted in the wild.

The four gardens profiled here are all actively involved in propagating and offering rare and unusual plants to the public. Taken as a whole, they serve as a fabulous horticultural resource. And yet, no two are alike. Each serves not only a different purpose but also demonstrates unique shade garden settings. In every case, those interested in growing easy care shade flowers will find stunning examples.

BOWMAN'S HILL WILDFLOWER PRESERVE
Washington Crossing, Pennsylvania

Most outstanding gardens are the horticultural expressions of strong-minded individuals, people with both the talent and the resources to transform their visions into masterpieces. Bowman's Hill Wildflower Preserve bears no such heritage. It is the beautiful result of a group effort, an 80-acre collection of plants brought into being by a large number of wildflower enthusiasts.

The setting was acquired in 1917 as a state park by Pennsylvania because of its historic interest: George Washington crossed the Delaware here and went on to trounce the Hessian soldiers in Trenton. Under state ownership, the former farmland slowly reverted back to a woodland setting carpeted with flowers.

Local wildflower admirers fell in love with the area. In the early 1930s, they installed the Bucks County Nature Trail. By the middle of that decade, they became even bolder. In 1934, they managed to convince the state to set aside an 80-acre portion of Washington Crossing Historic Park as a wildflower preserve. It was named for a well-known American Revolution lookout, Bowman's Hill.

In one sense, the Bucks County wildflower lovers got more than they asked for. With state sponsorship, the scope of the flora under the Preserve's purview was broadened to include examples of native habitats throughout Pennsylvania.

This is a tall order, for Pennsylvania's over 45,000 square miles climb from the waters of the Delaware over the Appalachian Mountains to the shores of Lake Erie, and encompass such disparate settings as dry remnant prairies, deep forests, and wet alkaline meadows. It is an instructive order, however, because it demonstrates that after initially creating the right habitat, gardeners can grow just about any plant without the use of fertilizers or pesticides.

In the case of Bowman's Hill, a tremendous amount of physical labor was needed to create the many different climate and geographical settings found in the state. Areas were made dry by raising them above surrounding levels; wet by lowering; acidic by adding sulfur; and moist and acidic by using Canadian peat instead of soil. In an area known as the Barrens, the needed low nutrient levels were obtained by trucking in quarry rock appropriate as a planting surface.

Currently, the Preserve contains 26 different trails, each reflecting a theme or specific plant setting. There is, for example, an Aster Walk, which is splendid in the fall; a Marshmarigold Trail, which explodes in a brilliant burst of color in spring; and an Audubon Trail, which is filled with berry-bearing plants. Fern lovers take special pleasure in walking along the trail originally planned and laid out by noted horticulturist Dr. Edgar T. Wherry.

There are approximately 900 species of wildflowers, shrubs, trees, and ferns throughout the Preserve. From March through October, visitors can find plants in bloom. In April, for example, ribbons of Virginia bluebells flood the appropriately named Bluebell Trail; in July, bloodred spires of cardinal flowers rise up; and in October, the golden yellow flowers of the common witch hazel shrub (*Hamamelis virginiana*) provide a glorious finale to the garden year.

The entire area is managed jointly by the Bowman's Hill Wildflower Preserve Association, Inc. (a nonprofit organization), the Washington Crossing Park Commission, and the Pennsylvania Historical and Museum Commission. As a further resource for the Preserve, a vast network of garden clubs sponsor various trails.

The Preserve's overall goal is to see its plants thrive with a minimum of assistance and expense within each carefully constructed habitat. Since plants coexist with diseases and insects in nature, these two garden headaches are not a significant problem in the Preserve. Aliens—in the form of nonnative plants and an inordinate number of deer—are.

The Fern Trail, almost luminous on a hot summer day, is one of 26 carefully grouped plant settings at Bowman's Hill Wildflower Preserve.

The lesser celandine (*Ranunculus ficaria*), for example, continually tries to shove aside the beautiful plants flowering on the Marshmarigold Trail. This problem—a choking, invasive spread of nonnative plants—is common throughout the U.S. While many American natives are being threatened with extinction by these invaders, the diligence of the Preserve's staff and volunteers protects its flowers.

The deer, however, are something else. With the residential development of the area surrounding Bowman's Hill and the disappearance of natural predators, deer herds have increased dramatically and have found a safe refuge within the Washington Crossing Historic Park. Nothing can be done to prevent their feeding on the many plants that have been so carefully collected and situated over the years. Bowman's Hill, according to museum educator Greg Edinger, was "fast

---

BOWMAN'S HILL WILDFLOWER PRESERVE
LIST OF EASY CARE SHADE FLOWERS

Spikenard (*Aralia racemosa*). Perennial with white flowers in summer and deep purple berries in fall.

Jack-in-the-Pulpit (*Arisaema triphyllum*). Perennial with green-striped hooded flower in spring and bright red berries in late summer.

Canadian Wild Ginger (*Asarum canadense*). Groundcover with inconspicuous purplish brown flowers in spring and velvety heart-shaped green leaves throughout the growing season.

Blue Cohosh (*Caulophyllum thalictroides*). Perennial with yellow-green flowers in spring and rich blue berries in fall.

Fringed Bleeding Heart (*Dicentra eximia*). Perennial with pink flowers late spring to fall.

Wild Geranium (*G. maculatum*). Perennial with blue-violet flowers in spring.

Mountain Laurel (*Kalmia latifolia*). Shrub with pink or white flowers in spring.

Cardinal Flower (*Lobelia cardinalis*). Perennial with scarlet flowers in late summer.

Trumpet Honeysuckle (*Lonicera sempervirens*). Vine with red, orange, or yellow flowers throughout summer.

Virginia Bluebells (*Mertensia virginica*). Perennial with pink buds opening to sky-blue flowers in early spring.

Partridge Berry (*Mitchella repens*). Groundcover with pinkish white tubular flowers in summer and red berries in winter.

Blue Woodland Phlox (*P. divaricata*). Perennial with light blue flowers in spring.

Creeping Phlox (*P. stolonifera*). Groundcover with blue, pink, white, or purple-violet flowers in spring.

Mayapple (*Podophyllum peltatum*). Groundcover with white flowers in spring.

American Jacob's Ladder (*Polemonium reptans*). Perennial with blue flowers in spring.

Flowering Raspberry (*Rubus odoratus*). Shrub with pinkish magenta flowers throughout summer.

Wreath Goldenrod (*Solidago caesia*). Perennial with yellow flowers in late summer.

Allegheny Foamflower (*Tiarella cordifolia*). Groundcover with white flowers in spring.

NOTE: The plants on this list were chosen by Greg Edinger, museum educator, and Tom Stevenson, plant propagator.

becoming a deer preserve rather than a wild-flower preserve." With a grant from the state, the Preserve is now being fenced in.

Under the overall direction of plant propagator Tom Stevenson, Bowman's Hill not only preserves plants but also makes them available to the general public. A large, ever-changing group of lovely, often hard-to-find flowers are on sale at the Plant Shop from April through October. For seed enthusiasts and those living in other parts of the country, the Preserve offers a mail-order program, providing seeds for many plants rarely offered in commercial trade.

> FOR FURTHER INFORMATION about membership and activities (including seed sales), write to Bowman's Hill Wildflower Preserve Association, Inc., Washington Crossing Historic Park, P.O. Box 103, Washington Crossing, PA 18977 (215/862–2924).

GARDEN IN THE WOODS
Framingham, Massachusetts

The Garden in the Woods is a dream come true. The dream belonged to Will C. Curtis, a landscape architect who used a superb artistic and esthetic sense as well as an admiration of native plants to create a horticultural masterpiece.

"There is quiet peace in it," he wrote. There is great beauty and magnificence as well. It is hard to realize that the carefully plotted trails, the scrupulously labeled plants, and the many garden settings across a glacially sculpted terrain of rolling hills, ponds, and streams were originally fashioned by this one man and his longtime assistant, Howard O. "Dick" Stiles. To this day, the Garden is one of our country's premier examples of how a low-maintenance, no-pesticide approach can result in a sumptuous floral setting with different plants in bloom from spring through fall.

Curtis bought the property, located about twenty-five miles west of Boston, in 1930 and then spent years clearing the land. Trails had to be carved and trees had to be removed to create planting areas and to allow the entrance of dappled sunlight. Chain saws were not available in those days; it would often take up to one week simply to down, chop, and remove a single maple.

In 1933, Dick Stiles—a young man with an innate love of and respect for plants—arrived on the scene. The two formed a lifelong partnership centered on the Garden. Curtis continued his landscaping practice, channeling all his income to the Garden. Stiles, with only a part-time helper, *maintained the entire area.* Thus, from the very beginning, the plants in the Garden were selected not only for good looks but also for ease of care. Pesticides were never used; leaf mulch and compost were always added to the soil each spring.

Although the habitat—soil, light, moisture conditions—for each plant was natural, the overall setting was not, for the Garden was always a landscaped one. Curtis loved floral beauty and applied his keen esthetic sense when grouping and placing plants.

A champion of native plants, Curtis also experimented with "foreigners," pairing plants from Asia with Americans that grew under similar climate conditions. This marriage of East and West is most visible in the Garden's woodland section, where he planted hostas, Asiatic rhododendrons (including *R. mucronulatum,* the Korean rhododendron), and the false anemone (*Anemonopsis macro-phylla*).

Propagation is another basic tenet of the Garden. At the time, Curtis wrote, this was an almost untrodden field. While by their very nature cultivars and hybrids were propagated, species plants—those occurring naturally in our woods and prairies—were simply collected in the wild. Even in the 1930s, however, it was evident that some plants were on the verge of extinction in their natural

Sprays of white wood aster tumble over a late-summer path at Garden in the Woods.

GARDEN IN THE WOODS
LIST OF EASY CARE SHADE FLOWERS

Jack-in-the-Pulpit (*Arisaema triphyllum*). Perennial with green-striped hooded flower in spring and bright red berries in late summer.

Canadian Wild Ginger (*Asarum canadense*). Groundcover with inconspicuous purplish brown flowers in spring and velvety heart-shaped green leaves throughout the growing season.

Black Cohosh (*Cimicifuga racemosa*). Perennial with candlelike spires of white flowers in summer.

Fringed Bleeding Heart (*Dicentra eximia*). Perennial with pink flowers late spring to fall.

Big Blue Lobelia (*L. siphilitica*). Perennial with blue or white flowers late summer into fall.

Partridge Berry (*Mitchella repens*). Groundcover with pinkish white tubular flowers in summer and red berries in winter.

Creeping Phlox (*P. stolonifera*). Groundcover with blue, pink, white, or purple-violet flowers in spring.

Small Solomon's Seal (*Polygonatum pubescens*). Perennial with graceful, arching stems featuring white bell-shaped flowers in spring and blue berries in late summer.

Bloodroot (*Sanguinaria canadensis*). Perennial with white flowers in early spring.

Allegheny Foamflower (*Tiarella cordifolia*). Groundcover with white flowers in spring.

Labrador Violet (*Viola labradorica* var. *purpurea*). Groundcover with purple flowers in spring and purple-tinged foliage throughout the growing season.

NOTE: This list was compiled by Heather McCargo, propagator at Garden in the Woods. "All of these shade plants," she writes, "are easy to grow in soil that has been enriched with leaf mold or compost."

habitats. Curtis felt it was ridiculous to tell people about beautiful plants they couldn't have; he opted for a positive approach in which he would demonstrate how many truly beautiful—and yet little known—flowers could be made available through commercial propagation.

For 34 years, Curtis and Stiles worked to realize their dream of a "big wildflower sanctuary in which plants will be grown, their likes and dislikes discovered, and the knowledge gained passed on in an effort to curb the wholesale destruction of our most beautiful natives."

By 1965, housing developers as well as companies anxious to exploit the sand and gravel deposits on the site threatened the property. At this time Curtis, over eighty years old, was unable to continue supporting the Garden in the Woods through his work. Turning down a $250,000 offer for the property, Curtis preserved his life's work by giving it to the New England Wild Flower Society.

Following Curtis's naturalistic style, the New England Wild Flower Society continues to develop the Garden in the Woods. Today, there are more than two miles of trails over the 45-acre property. Nearly 1,500 wildflowers, trees, shrubs, and grasses are displayed.

Perhaps the modern addition that would most please Curtis is the 1,000-square-foot passive solar greenhouse. Extensive experimentation on wildflower propagation is conducted in this facility. In addition, plants are raised, many of them extremely rare, and made available at the nursery shop throughout the growing season. For those who live too far away to buy such plants (there is no plant mail order program), the Garden in the Woods provides an extensive seed list filled with unusual, good-looking, low-maintenance offerings.

> FOR FURTHER INFORMATION about Garden in the Woods and its mail order seed program, write the New England Wild Flower Society, 180 Hemenway Road, Framingham, MA 01701–2699 (617/237–4924 or 508/877–7630). Two Society publications offer information about cultivating and propagating native plants; these are *Garden in the Woods Cultivation Guide* and *Propagation of Wildflowers* (revised by William E. Brumback). For further reading about Will Curtis and the founding of the Garden, see Margaret Hensel's excellent article in the May 1981 issue of *Horticulture* magazine.

THE RHODODENDRON SPECIES FOUNDATION
Federal Way, Washington

Gardening is such an all-encompassing activity that it can include dilettantes as well as fanatics. The latter, however, are politely referred to as plantsmen or, in today's more liberated times, as plantspersons. These are individuals who passionately hunger for new and unusual plants.

With an estimated hundreds of thousands of plants yet to be classified, such a quest can be daunting. As a result, many plantspersons have restricted their search for knowledge to one genus. This has given rise to several plant societies, of which the American Rhododendron Society (ARS) is among the more prominent.

Even though ARS members focus on a single shrub genus, they are still confronted with an estimated 850 different species. The rhododendron pool, however, is still larger, for each species usually comes in many different forms

Courtesy of The Rhododendron Species Foundation

(the last expression, in nonhorticultural terms, is used to distinguish the physical differences between closely related plants; for example, two "sisters" distinctly varying in height or color can be called forms).

When the number of species is combined with the estimated number of forms, the result is literally thousands of very different rhododendrons. These come in sizes to fit any landscape, from the short, 3-foot-tall coast azalea (*R. atlanticum*), which is perfect for small gardens, to the giant, 50-foot tree rhododendron (*R. arboreum*), which is magnificent on grand estates. (Though most gardeners distinguish between azaleas and rhododendrons, botanists classify them in the same genus. Generally, small-leaved, deciduous rhododendrons with open, saucer-shaped flowers are called azaleas.)

The garden at The Rhododendron Species Foundation has a continuous succession of rhododendron bloom from late January to July. Here the white flowers of a native dogwood look elegant with the lavender extravaganza of R. polycladum.

Given that rhododendrons not only vary in size and leaf form but also bear flowers in many shapes and colors, it is not surprising that David Leach wrote in his definitive book, *Rhododendrons of the World*, that rhododendrons are the "most varied and unwieldy group of plants that exist on this earth."

THE RHODODENDRON SPECIES FOUNDATION
LIST OF EASY CARE RHODODENDRONS

Coast Azalea (*R. atlanticum*). Small 3-foot shrub with fragrant white or light pink flowers in late spring. Spreading by runners, this is one of the very few stoloniferous azaleas. Hardy to −10°F.

Catawba Rhododendron (*R. catawbiense*). Evergreen native of the Great Smoky Mountains, 6 feet to 18 feet tall, with lilac purple or white flowers in late spring. Hardy to −25°F.

Rhododendron concinnum. A little known twiggy shrub, this rhododendron grows up to 7 feet and is covered with purple to reddish purple flowers in spring. Hardy to −5°F.

Dahurian Rhododendron. (*R. dauricum*). Short (4 feet to 5 feet) and deciduous with purple, pink, or white flowers, this is one of the earliest rhododendrons to bloom. Hardy to −25°F.

Cloudland Rhododendron (*R. impeditum*). Good rock garden plant (only 1 foot high) with blue flowers in April and May. Hardy to −25°F.

Kyushu Azalea (*R. kiusianum*). Semi-evergreen, 3-foot-tall shrub with flowers in purple, white, pink, salmon, or crimson in May. One of the parents of a group of azaleas known as Kurume Hybrids. Hardy to −5°F.

Pontic Azalea (*R. luteum*). Deciduous shrub, 6 feet to 12 feet, with fragrant yellow flowers in May. A favorite of British garden designer Gertrude Jekyll, who included it in her garden at Munstead Wood. One of the parents of a group of azaleas known as Ghent Hybrids. Hardy to −25°F.

Ponticum Rhododendron (*R. ponticum*). Densely branched, evergreen shrub, 15 feet tall, with purple-pink flowers in June. Often seen as a pruned hedge in the British Isles, where it is naturalized. Hardy to 0°F.

R. pseudochrysanthemum. Originally collected in 1918 in the conifer forests of Mount Morrison on Taiwan by the famous plant explorer E. H. Wilson; rediscovered by John Creech while on a 1967 plant expedition for the U.S. National Arboretum. Low-growing (1 foot to 10 feet tall) and interesting shrub bearing pink, white tinged with pink, or white flowers in April. Hardy to −5°F.

Royal Alp Rhododendron (*R. russatum*). Small (2 feet to 4 feet), floriferous alpine with blue-purple flowers in April. Needs alpine conditions—cool summer temperatures and a moist atmosphere. Hardy to −10°F.

Williams Rhododendron (*R. williamsianum*). A 5-foot-tall plant grown for its foliage (heart-shaped leaves that are initially bronze-colored and then turn a bluish-green) as well as its pink flowers, which open in April. Hardy to 0°F.

Rhododendron yakushimanum. A recently introduced Japanese species, this plant is a short (3 feet to 4 feet), slow-growing shrub with handsome evergreen foliage. In spring it is covered with pink or rose-colored buds that open into white flowers. Hardy to −20°F.

NOTE: The above rhododendrons were selected by the Foundation as being the most hardy and beautiful beginner plants.

ARS members, of course, also think they are among the most beautiful. But prejudiced as they are, these members also readily acknowledge that some rhododendrons are lovelier than others. Therefore, it was with great concern that a group belonging to an Oregon chapter noticed that many inferior rhododendron forms were being propagated and foisted off on an American public that had just begun to take a keen interest in gardening.

The time was the early 1960s. These same rhododendron devotees were also aware that several rhododendron collections in British gardens were being reduced due to financial constraints. Many of these plants were the direct descendants of those gathered by plant explorers in Asia (the Himalayas are the most abundant source for members of the genus) during the late 1800s and early 1900s. Men had risked, and at times, lost, their lives to obtain these exquisite plants.

The decision was made to start The Rhododendron Species Foundation; its mission would be to preserve the finest form of every known rhododendron and to make these choice forms available to gardeners throughout the world.

From its initial founding to this day, an extraordinary amount of personal commitment and institutional generosity has underlain the workings of The Rhododendron Species Foundation. Dr. Milton Walker, of Eugene, Oregon, for example, traveled many times—at his own expense—to England and Scotland looking for superior rhododendron forms to serve as the nucleus of The Rhododendron Species Foundation. Private and public British botanical gardens donated scions of their best plants to inaugurate the collection.

Dr. Walker, as well as P. H. Brydon (former director of San Francisco's Strybing Arboretum), originally cared for the collections on their own properties. When the number of plants neared 3,000, however, it was obvious that the scope of the collection was too large for any one individual to care for.

Enter the Weyerhaeuser Company. In a 1974 offer dubbed "unprecedented in the annals of American horticulture," the firm offered to lend the Foundation 24 acres of land on its headquarters in Federal Way, Washington (about halfway between Tacoma and Seattle). Since that time, the Foundation's administrators have created one of the most diverse and complete collections of species rhododendrons in the world, with over 8,500 superior plants representing the finest forms of approximately 500 species.

With its gardens open year-round, the Foundation fulfills its educational mission by allowing visitors to see stunning examples of rhododendron beauty. Through on-site plant sales, the Foundation offers up to 500 different kinds of rhododendrons, the vast majority of which are not available elsewhere. Rhododendron plants are also offered to Foundation members through the mail. Thus, shade gardeners throughout the country now have an almost limitless choice of rare and beautiful examples of this multifaceted genus for their own beds.

FOR FURTHER INFORMATION about the Found[ation], write to The Rhododendron Sp[ecies] Foundation, P.O. Box 3798, Federal W[ay,] 98063-3798 (206/838–4646).

WINTERTHUR GARDEN
Winterthur, Delaware

That last name—du Pont—tells you something. It means money, lots of it. And Henry Francis du Pont, upon inheriting his family's estate at Winterthur, was an extremely wealthy man. He was also a horticultural expert, one of the few moneyed aristocrats in our nation's history to have training in the field.

These two conditions alone—wealth and horticultural expertise—would guarantee the creation of a garden of interest. Du Pont, however, possessed yet another quality: a keen esthetic sense.

This was the man who would have his chief gardener bring him the finest blooming flower from the cutting garden each morning. On the basis of that flower's color and form, du Pont would then choose the china pattern for the day.

This was also the man who would have the draperies and slipcovers in many rooms changed four times a year. Research by Denise Magnani, Winterthur Curator and Director of Landscape Division, indicates that the seasonal colors of the fabrics echoed that of the blooming flowers viewed from the windows of the house.

Winterthur Garden, then, is special. It was designed to exhibit plants in a setting of unri-
̇ ̣ ̣racious beauty. Swaths of carefully cho-
-binations stream across the
̇̇̇ng when the Garden

of 985 acres, of
̣ed. That is a lot
̣rvised just about
picking plants for
̣y surprise some—
̣taff of 100, du Pont
̣mperamental plants
̣ork and that could die

and ruin a carefully plotted color scheme.

Thus, amidst rare exotics and Winterthur-bred cultivars, one will also find such old garden staples as tawny daylilies (*Hemerocallis fulva*), blue hostas (*Hosta ventricosa*), and wild hydrangeas (*H. arborescens* and *H. arborescens* 'Grandiflora'). Mass groupings of these plants have survived for decades without any special care.

After studying at Harvard's horticulture school, the now-defunct Bussey Institution, du Pont returned home and began to put his learning to work. The March Bank, begun in 1902, is Winterthur's oldest existing garden area. It beautifully reflects his attempt to incorporate the philosophy of two prominent English gardeners: Gertrude Jekyll, who pioneered the artistic use of color, and William Robinson, who championed growing perennials outside of formal borders. Thousands of bulbs were planted in this area, flooding the spring ground with blues, yellows, and whites.

Du Pont went on to create many garden areas. Today there are eleven designated sites on the estate grounds. Two of these—the Reflecting Pool Garden and the Sundial Garden—are bathed in sunshine and were designed by landscape architect Marian Coffin, a personal friend.

The nine other garden areas are filled with woodland shade. Though informal, they were planned with minute precision by du Pont. He was particularly concerned with blooming sequence, wanting—as do all gardeners—to stretch out the flowering period as long as possible. For example, as the billowing, light blue woodland phlox begins to fade, the color is picked up by a flow of Spanish squill (*Endymion*

hispanicus) scattered among the phlox.

It has been written that such precision results in an emotionally cool garden, that no spontaneity takes place. This is not true. The Italian windflower, for example, appeared mysteriously one year in the area known as the Azalea Woods. There is speculation that a few tubers were tucked in one of the azalea root balls; they sprouted, and were so happy with their surroundings that they proceeded to multiply and spread in a variety of colors from white to blue throughout that area.

Though his designs and color combinations still attract awe and admiration, du Pont's chief contribution to gardeners everywhere was his evaluation, introduction, and nurture of elegant low-maintenance plants. Each species that came to his attention was carefully examined for color, hardiness, and bloom period before being officially placed on the estate grounds. Often a plant would remain in a testing area for three years before being deemed worthy for the Garden.

Du Pont had the resources to search the world for plant treasures, and he did so. The fernleaf corydalis, for example, is a Chinese native that was purchased in the early 1930s. Its original use was as landscaping material on some rocky banks. The plants settled in, were somewhat forgotten as other projects took priority, and thrived untended for nearly three decades.

They were "rediscovered" when the eighty-one-year-old du Pont decided to develop the Quarry Garden in 1961. What a plant gem to come across! While the flowers add charm to early spring gardens with their 8-inch bright yellow spikes, the major attraction of this perennial is its rich, fernlike foliage. It is finer, neater, and better-looking than that of many a true fern. Without du Pont's interest, this plant would probably still be unknown to American gardens.

When he died in 1969, du Pont left a collection that combined rare specimens of individual

Linda Eirhart

Visitors to Winterthur today can still appreciate the sentiment expressed by Henry Francis du Pont in a 1944 letter: "… I wish you could see my spring bank — it is just one sheet of Chionodoxa luciliae.*"*

plants with mass groupings of carefree bulbs and perennials; the whole formed one of the most beautiful and successful naturalistic gardens in the world. Under the auspices of the Winterthur staff, these collections are maintained, and through its nursery many of the rare and lovely plants that du Pont introduced are available to gardeners throughout our country.

FOR FURTHER INFORMATION about Winterthur Garden, see Harold H. Bruce's *Winterthur in Bloom*, published by Winterthur and available through the Winterthur Garden Shop. For visitor information, phone (800) 448-3883. For a copy of the Winterthur Gift and Garden Sampler catalogue, phone (800) 767-0500.

WINTERTHUR GARDEN
LIST OF EASY CARE SHADE FLOWERS

Pheasant's-eye (*Adonis amurensis*). Perennial with shiny, brilliant yellow cup flowers in late winter.

Italian Windflower (*Anemone apennina*). Tuber with flowers ranging from blue to white in early spring.

Glory-of-the-Snow (*Chionodoxa luciliae*). Bulb with blue flowers in early spring.

Lily-of-the-Valley (*Convallaria majalis*). Perennial with fragrant white flowers in spring.

Fernleaf Corydalis (*C. cheilanthifolia*). Perennial with yellow flowers in spring.

Winterhazel (*Corylopsis* 'Winterthur'). Shrub with pale yellow flowers in early spring.

Lenten Rose (*Helleborus orientalis*). Perennial with flowers in delicate white, pink, purple, or green tones in early spring.

Virginia Bluebells (*Mertensia virginica*). Perennial with pink buds opening to sky-blue flowers in early spring.

Blue Woodland Phlox (*P. divaricata*). Perennial with light blue flowers in spring.

Japanese Primrose (*Primula japonica*). Perennial with delicate crimson, pink, or white blossoms in spring.

Snow Azalea (*Rhododendron mucronatum* 'Winterthur'). Shrub with clear lavender flowers in spring.

Korean Rhododendron (*R. mucronulatum*). Shrub with pale lavender flowers in early spring.

Chapter Four

PRIVATE GARDENS

Yellow goldenstar, pink Lancaster geranium, and white crested iris bloom in the dappled shade of an early May border at Marnie Flook's Chestertown, Maryland, home.

In one sense, growing flowers is the easiest leisure activity possible. Since there are absolutely no rules as to how much time or effort is required, it is essentially whatever the gardener makes of it. This aspect of gardening is highlighted in the four shade gardens described in this chapter.

Gay Bumgarner, for example, created a simple but lovely no-maintenance garden in the woods filling her backyard in Columbus, Missouri. Linda Yang, on the other hand, has packed a lifetime of memories, a plethora of design styles, and an extensive plant collection into her Manhattan flower beds. Jan Plenty, who

originally thought plants only flowered in sun, has had to cope with salt air and snails in cultivating shade gardens at The Old Milano Hotel on California's Mendocino coast. And a series of moves has led to Marnie Flook's learning to garden successfully in a large wooded property; in a small townhouse yard; and now on a Chestertown, Maryland, riverbank.

Each garden is very different and yet each quite lovely—just as yours will be once you have finished reading about the experiences of these four individuals and have considered their plant recommendations.

GAY BUMGARNER'S WOODLAND GARDEN
Columbia, Missouri

Gay Bumgarner is a professional nature photographer. If you subscribe to garden magazines or buy Sierra Club or Audubon calendars, you have probably seen her pictures.

Bumgarner not only likes to photograph but also to look at nature, particularly through the windows of her own home. When she and her husband bought a house in 1976, Bumgarner decided to transform her 90-by-90-foot wooded backyard into a completely maintenance-free garden, one with something of visual interest throughout the year.

Low maintenance is one thing, no maintenance another. In order to achieve the latter, a good deal of prior work—in terms of both research and physical labor—is required.

Bumgarner first plotted a simple design scheme. She decided to create a meandering path through the center of the property, placing it so that the end could not be seen at the start of the woods. This path would then split near the property line, with each fork forming a loop around the edge of the woods and leading back to the house. Each loop, she decided, would comprise a walkway, circling woods filled with small trees, understory shrubs, and flowers— some to be grouped for color and bloom period and others to be allowed to roam at will.

She then noted the natural setting of her yard. The land sloped down and the limestone soil was quite rocky. A longtime resident of Columbia, she was all too familiar with its warm, wet springs and then bone-dry, blistering hot summers. Winter temperatures can drop as low as –10°F.

Thus, she knew she had to choose plants that would withstand wide temperature fluctuations, help prevent soil erosion, and thrive in shade. There was one other very important consideration: she also wanted plants that would produce berries for birds.

For inspiration, she took walks through nearby Missouri woods. There she would note what plants were thriving unattended and under conditions similar to that of her backyard. Her reasoning was simple and logical: duplicate the habitat and let nature take its course.

Next, she took stock of what was already growing on her property. Periwinkle was well on its way to providing a light blanket for the entire woods. There were also early-blooming bulbs—winter aconite, Siberian squill, and daffodils.

While there were several native dogwoods, there were few understory shrubs. Bumgarner decided to install burning bushes, shrubs noted not only for their brilliant red fall foliage but also for their berries, which attract numerous birds. Berries that remain uneaten germinate profusely, and within several years the woods became filled with these shrubs.

Planting was extremely difficult and laborious. To begin, there were lots of rocks and roots. Land had to be cleared for each plant; that meant digging out rocks and replacing them with buckets of soil. She did not begrudge this effort, because she knew that once she had properly planted a shrub or flower she would never again need to care for it.

She devoted the greater part of her effort to "formalizing" the initial part of the central path. Here she planted hostas, Virginia bluebells, Dutchman's breeches, daffodils, and surprise

Gay Bumgarner

Using carefully chosen plants, Gay Bumgarner created a no-maintenance garden in Columbia, Missouri. In this picture, taken in early spring, daffodils beckon visitors to walk down the entrance pathway. In the bottom right corner, Dutchman's breeches lead off the flower parade. For a look at this garden 3 months later, see page 46.

Gay Bumgarner

In early August, colorful surprise lilies pop up through a thick green groundcover of periwinkle in Gay Bumgarner's no-maintenance garden (see page 45 for a look at this garden 3 months earlier).

lilies (*Amaryllis belladonna*). These formed a flowering escort, inviting visitors and Bumgarner herself to stroll further into the garden and explore the rest of its natural beauty.

One of her best choices was the false Solomon's seal. Though this native is supposed to prefer moist soils, it didn't seem to mind the dry Missouri summers. Happily nestled within the leaf mulch of Bumgarner's woods, it spouted feathery white panicles of flowers every spring and then dangled attractive red berries from its arching stems. The birds were so attracted to the berries that the plants had little opportunity to seed themselves. Bumgarner bought lots more, enough to ensure their spread throughout the woods.

There were also some failures. Native bleeding hearts (*Dicentra eximia*) were uncomfortable during summer droughts. On the other hand, their close cousins—Dutchman's breeches—settled right in without any adjustment problems.

And there were also surprises. Wild geraniums appeared (a gift from the birds, she believes) and flourished in mass groupings. Tawny daylilies arrived and took over one corner. The delicate pink flowers of the spring beauty popped up among the periwinkle and proceeded to multiply freely. Virginia bluebells bobbed up and down with the early spring breezes drifting through the woods.

Bumgarner found it necessary to water—particularly the shrubs—the first few years of her garden. After about four years, her part in the garden's life disappeared. There were no pesticides, no fertilizers, no waterings. Falling leaves provided mulch and, eventually, compost. If a flower wasn't acclimated, it simply disappeared; there were enough others to take its place.

For over ten years, with absolutely no maintenance whatsoever, Bumgarner looked at a lovely scene of changing beauty. In the winter, the evergreen leaves of the periwinkle and the last berries of the burning bush added a touch of color. By late February, the cheery yellow blossoms of winter aconite began to appear, to be quickly followed by the tide of color formed by the spring perennials and the carpet of blue flowers on the vinca.

In summer, the orange daylily flowers would fill one corner. Several weeks later the lovely blossoms of the surprise lily would stand as white and pink guards of honor along the dark green of the woodland path. And then, in fall, the bright red of the burning bush would join the gorgeous parade of all the golden, orange, and crimson forest leaves floating idly to the ground.

Bumgarner and her husband have since built a house on acreage in the country. She is so busy taking pictures—shooting, filing, and marketing hundreds upon hundreds of slides—that she has yet to find the hours to become an involved gardener. And yet, for one who loves nature, the idea of being without a garden represents a personal loss. Thus, having so beautifully demonstrated the possibilities of a no-maintenance shade garden, she is now devising a strategy for a similar endeavor in the sun.

> FOR FURTHER INFORMATION as well as additional pictures of Gay Bumgarner's garden, see the September/October 1990 issue of *Fine Gardening* magazine. *Fine Gardening* is a reader-written publication and often features first-person descriptions of shade gardens and how they came into being. For subscription or back-issue information, call (800) 283-7252.

GAY BUMGARNER
LIST OF EASY CARE SHADE FLOWERS

Surprise Lily (*Amaryllis belladonna*). Bulb with rose, pink, purple, or white flowers in summer.

Spring Beauty (*Claytonia virginica*). Corm with palest pink flowers in spring.

Dutchman's Breeches (*Dicentra cucullaria*). Perennial with white flowers in spring.

Winter Aconite (*Eranthis hyemalis*). Tuber with bright yellow flowers in late winter.

Burning Bush (*Euonymus alata*). Shrub with inconspicuous purple flowers in spring and brilliant red foliage in fall.

Wild Geranium (*G. maculatum*). Perennial with blue-violet flowers in spring.

Tawny Daylily (*Hemerocallis fulva*). Perennial with orange flowers in summer.

Virginia Bluebells (*Mertensia virginica*). Perennial with pink buds opening to sky-blue flowers in early spring.

Siberian Squill (*Scilla siberica*). Bulb with bright blue flowers in late winter.

False Solomon's Seal (*Smilacina racemosa*). Perennial with white flowers in spring.

Periwinkle (*Vinca minor*). Groundcover with blue flowers in spring.

MARNIE FLOOK'S THIRD GARDEN

Chestertown, Maryland

Marnie Flook, now gardening on the Chester River in Maryland, has bid farewell to two superb gardens, and is currently working on her third.

The first was in Greenville, Delaware, where she and her husband, Bill, moved in 1955. Two bare retaining walls had been built on the sloping, wooded three acres. When Flook decided to tuck flowers among the unadorned rocks, her search for appropriate plants led her down a specialized path that is open to any gardener choosing to follow it.

She enrolled in courses at Longwood Gardens, joined horticultural and plant societies, and traveled extensively to see and photograph plants in natural settings. Since there were few commercial nurseries at that time offering rock-garden plants, she started raising her own from seed. Many were rare and unusual flowers, obtained through the seed exchanges offered by the American Rock Garden Society (ARGS).

Society membership was a source not only of seeds but also of friendships with many gardeners, including prominent horticulturist Edgar T. Wherry, who discovered one of Flook's favorite shade flowers—the pink Foamflower. Originally named as *Tiarella wherryi*, this spring charmer with spikes of soft pink or white blossoms has since been reclassified as *Tiarella cordifolia* var. *wherryi*. "To me," Flook says, "the plant will always be *Tiarella wherryi*."

While she was culling information from various sources, she was repaying with donations of her time and her experience-based knowledge. She joined the ARGS board and then that of Longwood Gardens. Flook also lectured, wrote articles for gardening publications, and served as editor of the *Brooklyn Botanic Garden Handbook on Rock Gardening.*

And then, so quickly it was hard to believe it had happened, the five children were grown and the large, comfortable house became simply too large. "The decision to move," Flook says, "was probably the most difficult we have ever made."

The relocation to a Wilmington townhouse in 1981 was perfect for empty nesters; the 25-foot by 35-foot backyard was a challenge to those who had planted on a large scale. After selecting a limited number of flowers and shrubs to take on the move, the Flooks had a group of raised beds constructed. Planted as miniature gardens, these substituted many of the features and advantages of the rock walls.

In giving up acres of flowers, Flook did gain hours to pursue other interests. Chief among these was joining her garden club members in archiving Henry Francis du Pont's garden papers at Winterthur. This work led to her meeting du Pont's curator of plants, Hal Bruce, before he died. Through him she learned about beautiful, newly introduced shade-thriving perennials and shrubs.

The Wilmington townhouse garden was much too sunny for these plants and Flook yearned to grow them in the family's two-acre, pie-shaped property bordering the Chester River. Her husband discouraged her, pointing out that weekend retreats at their cottage would become weekend workouts if new gardens were installed.

With severe dry spells demonstrating the futility of trying to water effectively a large area, the Flooks have restricted the size of their flower beds. Careful design, incorporating the use of tall shrubs backed by looming trees, makes this small shaded area look much larger than it actually is.

After deciding to make this location their retirement home, however, garden activity in Maryland began in earnest. One of their first projects was to have raised beds built; the Flooks had been extremely pleased with this form of gardening in Wilmington.

There was now ample room to garden in the shade. One of the first raised beds was placed under the leafy umbrella of a towering elm tree. In planting this bed, Flook was filled with happy memories of her Greenville days, where leaves from oaks, tulip poplars, and beeches formed a rich and organic soil and the tree roots allowed space for wildflowers to flourish.

What a shock to discover a year later that roots from the elm tree had crept in and almost completely filled the planter. Flook had never gardened amongst such tentacles. "It was a humbling experience," she admits.

It was grueling for Bill Flook. He dug out the bed, severed all the roots, laid down black plastic (with holes punched in for drainage), increased the height of the bed, and then replanted all the shrubs and perennials. The tree—which had already shown signs of illness—perversely responded by dying, leaving all the shade plants in almost full sun.

Some people would view the situation as a disaster. A gardener looks at it as an opportunity to create another planting area, and that is exactly what the Flooks did. A wooded side of the property was partially cleared to make room for the shade flowers.

Two of the many plants in this setting are old favorites: dwarf hostas, grown from seed collected from plants originally moved from Greenville to Wilmington, and the white-flowered epimedium, treasured not only for its dainty spring flowers but also for its beautiful, long-lasting leaves. These epimediums are second generation cuttings, with the originals growing in Greenville and the first cuttings in the Wilmington townhouse.

MARNIE FLOOK
LIST OF EASY CARE SHADE FLOWERS

American Columbine (*Aquilegia canadensis*). Perennial with red and yellow flowers in spring.

European Wild Ginger (*Asarum europaeum*). Groundcover with inconspicuous brown flowers in spring and rich, dark, shiny green foliage throughout the growing season.

'Pumila' Astilbe (*A. chinensis* 'Pumila'). Perennial with raspberry pink flowers in summer.

Goldenstar (*Chrysogonum virginianum*). Groundcover with yellow flowers in spring, summer, and often into fall.

Fringed Bleeding Heart (*Dicentra eximia*). Perennial with pink flowers late spring to fall.

White Epimedium (*E. x youngianum* 'Niveum'). Perennial with white flowers in spring.

Sweet Woodruff (*Galium odoratum* but also listed and sold as *Asperula odorata*). Groundcover with white flowers in spring.

Coral Bells (*Heuchera sanguinea*). Perennial with pink flowers late spring into summer.

Dwarf Hosta (*H. venusta*). Perennial with lilac flowers in summer.

Allegheny Foamflower (*Tiarella cordifolia*). Groundcover with white flowers in spring.

Pink Foamflower (*Tiarella cordifolia* var. *wherryi*). Perennial with white or pale pink flowers in spring.

The Chestertown garden reflects lessons learned from the two previous gardens. The temptation to expand indefinitely is being resisted, a task made easier by recent droughts, which have demonstrated all too vividly the futility of effectively watering a large garden area.

Easy care flowers, many from shady Greenville days, are being reintroduced, among them the 'Pumila' astilbe. "Its raspberry pink plumes appear in August when most plants are not in flower," Flook notes. "As an added bonus, the dry stalks provide winter interest."

Though the Flooks have said goodbye to two gardens and are in the process of creating a totally new one, there is one factor that has remained constant: they do a really good job. As the Greenville and Wilmington gardens were, the Chestertown garden is often featured on tours offered by plant societies and horticultural organizations.

Not shown on such tours are the stacks of papers inside the house, for Marnie Flook is now involved in a new endeavor: archiving the extensive material of the American Rock Garden Society. Gardening, after all, is what you make of it. Through her explorations in botany, horticulture, and history as well as her role as an educator and volunteer, Flook has more than demonstrated how enriching an activity it can be.

FOR FURTHER INFORMATION about membership in the American Rock Garden Society and participation in its seed exchange, write: Secretary, ARGS, P.O. Box 67, Millwood, NY 10546.

THE OLD MILANO HOTEL'S MENDOCINO COAST GARDEN
Gualala, California

Coastal Californians, particularly those living in the northern half of the state, have to deal with an unusual cause of shade: summer fog—thick gray miasmas of it drawn from the ocean by the intense heat of the inland Sacramento Valley.

The little town of Gualala, perched on the spectacular rocky shores along the southern Mendocino coast, is fortunate to escape much of this gray summer blanket. It's easier to grow shade plants here precisely because sunnier days are more frequent, days in which the three to five hours of sun slipping under tree-covered areas or beaming down on northern corners of buildings can be fully utilized by plants.

In winter, however, Gualala shares the same weather as its neighboring towns: temperatures down in the 20s and at least one annual snowstorm. Snails—the bane of California gardens—and gophers are longtime settlers in the area. Gardening here, as everywhere, can be a challenge.

To the many Victorian inns dotted along the Mendocino coastline, gardening is a must. Colorful flowers add a cozy charm to these small establishments, a personal touch that distinguishes bed-and-breakfast inns from competing hotel and motel chains.

Thus, one of the first decisions Leslie Linscheid made when she bought The Old Milano Hotel in 1984 was to expand the gardens. She hired Jan Plenty, who had been landscaping at another inn, and gave her the following goals:

1 Create low-maintenance gardens. The intimate hotel is not large enough to support a full-time grounds crew on its three acres of property.

2 Offer a sense of privacy as well as a feeling that guests are escaping from the busy demands of their lifestyles; many are metropolitan residents of the San Francisco Bay area, 100 miles to the south.

3 Exhibit year-round interest. Recent temperature lows in the 20s have made this last goal particularly difficult.

The Old Milano Hotel grounds include both sunny and shaded areas. Jan Plenty's experience with sun-flowering plants was both professional and personal. Her own house is perched on the ocean; there she has a "postage-stamp-size garden," in which she experiments with plants that can withstand the wind and salt air of the Mendocino coast.

At the time she was hired by Linscheid, however, Plenty had never gardened in shaded surroundings. "Like most people," she admits, "I thought plants only flowered in the sun." Fortunately, the shaded areas on The Old Milano Hotel grounds are in the back of the building. While all the plants have to cope with salt air, strong ocean winds are not a major problem. In addition, the soil is excellent, well drained and rich in organic matter.

Though Plenty initially relied on the recommendations of local nurseries for shade-tolerant plants, she soon began to build up a large garden library. As is true of many gardeners, she enjoys searching for just the right plant almost as much as she does cultivating one.

Plenty spent her first years at The Old Milano Hotel not only maintaining the existing gar-

Judy Jakobsen

Red nasturtiums, plus white and pink Japanese hybrid anemones, form a colorful October backdrop to a quiet resting spot at The Old Milano Hotel.

dens but also creating several new ones, all tucked away in different areas of the property. Along with the additional garden areas, however, came additional goals:

1 The gardens now serve not only as an attraction outside but also provide decorative flowers inside, especially in the restaurant, which draws many day visitors as well as overnight guests.

2 Pesticides are banned. Many of the flowers are used as entree garnishes and in salads (the nasturtiums, for example, are a pungent and colorful addition to green salads).

3 Guests are allowed to take cuttings or slips for replanting in their homes. Thus the plants cannot be rare exotic species that would be too expensive to share with others.

In addition to the quirks of weather, the need for constant floral cutting, and the heavily used aspect of the gardens, Plenty has had to take into account two more factors: snails and gophers.

She has worked out a peaceful coexistence with the latter: the gophers are allowed free run of the lawn, while any flowers that they are particularly fond of, such as tulips, are placed in pots.

Snails are held at bay naturally during the drought of summer and the cold of winter. In the cooler, wetter weather of spring and fall—conditions under which they revel—Plenty spends a lot of time handpicking the creatures. And since snails are averse to the tannin in newly cut wood, Plenty uses a fresh supply of bark chips every year as a mulch. She reports that a friend has switched to redwood chips and swears that he hasn't seen one snail since he started using them.

Plant stalwarts form a colorful backbone for the shade gardens. These include hellebores, grape hyacinths, foxgloves, cinerarias, and

THE OLD MILANO HOTEL
LIST OF EASY CARE SHADE FLOWERS

'Peter Pan' Agapanthus (*A. cultivar*). Bulb with blue flowers in summer.

Japanese Anemone (*A. x hybrida*). Perennial with white to many shades of pink flowers in fall.

Tuberous Begonia (*B. x tuberhybrida*). Tuber with lustrous red, yellow, white, pink, or orange flowers late spring to frost.

Foxglove (*Digitalis purpurea*). Biennial with white to deep pink flowers in late spring.

Corsican Hellebore (*Helleborus lividus* subsp. *corsicus;* often listed and sold as *H. argutifolius*). Perennial with long-lasting green flowers that first open in early spring.

Christmas Rose (*Helleborus niger*). Perennial with white flowers in winter.

Lenten Rose (*Helleborus orientalis*). Perennial with flowers in delicate white, pink, purple, or green tones in early spring.

Grape Hyacinth (*Muscari botryoides*). Bulb with blue flowers in late winter and early spring.

Japanese Andromeda (*Pieris japonica*). Shrub with drooping clusters of white flowers in spring.

Cineraria (*Senecio x hybridus*). Annual with white, pink, red, blue, or purple flowers all summer.

Nasturtium (*Tropaeolum majus*). Annual with red, orange, or yellow flowers summer to frost.

Japanese anemones. All are drought-resistant, an increasingly important factor in California gardens.

In the summer, self-seeded nasturtiums appear everywhere. "They're almost a weed here," Plenty explains. She lets them wander through the shade garden because she doesn't want to take the time to pull them out and because they provide quite a bit of color.

Though Plenty has her "regulars," additions and surprise appearances ensure that her gardens are never the same from year to year. Yellow tuberous begonias, for example, recently confounded horticultural literature by surviving a winter of snow and freezing temperatures and popping up again the following summer.

Many new gardeners feel that it's difficult to have flower color in a shaded setting. As Jan Plenty has learned and now demonstrates to guests at The Old Milano Hotel, low-maintenance shade gardens are not only practical and feasible but also are quite lovely all year long.

FOR FURTHER INFORMATION about The Old Milano Hotel and its gardens, write Leslie L. Linscheid, 38300 Highway One, Gualala, California 95445, or call (707) 884-3256.

LINDA YANG'S CITY GARDEN
New York, New York

Linda Yang is a born and bred city gardener. From the time she was a little girl watching her father prune an immense magnolia in his Brooklyn front yard through heady days on Manhattan balconies and rooftops down to her current city townhouse, she has always known about gardening in small spaces.

As a *New York Times* garden columnist and author of two books, she has written that she loves being a city gardener, that she hankers not one bit for any greener pastures. That's not quite true, however; Linda Yang wants those pastures but she wants them in the city.

She wants an English perennial border, a woodland glen, a formal herb garden, a splashing water oasis, a bamboo stand, a tranquil green moss patch, and a rock garden. Using creativity, determination, extensive research, and hours of really dirty work, she has pulled it off.

Her father sparked her initial interest in gardening. One of her fondest childhood memories is watching him tend his brilliant red climbing roses. On warm summer evenings he would cut clusters of these and place them in a shiny black vase.

Though losing a yard when she left home, Yang carried on the family garden tradition with potted plants, both indoors and out. Just when the balcony on her first apartment was filled to overflowing, she and her husband moved, acquiring a rooftop with their new quarters. To a city girl it was like inheriting a vast estate.

To make sure her mistakes were not in the same proportion, Yang took classes at the Brooklyn Botanic Garden and conducted plant and design research in the library of the Horticultural Society of New York. There she had the good fortune to meet the legendary Elizabeth C. Hall, the Society's senior librarian.

Miss Hall (no one ever, to public knowledge, called her Elizabeth) was warm, witty, and wonderful. And she charmed Linda Yang as she charmed the thousands of gardeners she helped throughout her ninety-plus years.

Miss Hall became a personal friend and steered Yang to a wealth of information resources. In reading and then experimenting herself, Yang became not only a good gardener but also an extremely knowledgeable one. In 1979 *The New York Times* asked her to write a garden column.

Then Yang discovered the dark side of the plant world. She moved from a bright sunny rooftop down to a townhouse with a yard surrounded by buildings stretching up to the sky.

Fortunately, Miss Hall introduced her to Harriet K. Morse and her book *Gardening in the Shade*, the first definitive, and for decades the only, work on the subject. Miss Hall had even helped Mrs. Morse with its research.

A series of at-home teas and luncheons followed, at first in Yang's townhouse and then, when increasing age prevented Mrs. Morse from climbing the front steps, at Mrs. Morse's apartment. The three would sit and animatedly talk in botanical Latin as they devoured food, shared plant lore, and cultivated friendship.

Yang started out with a city grass lot 18 feet wide and 50 feet deep. Most shade gardens have some inherent structure—whether it be a wall or

a tree—that provides shade. Yang had only a neighbor's tree and tall buildings that surrounded her garden space but were not part of it.

The initial outlook, then, was quite bleak. The ground was even more of a problem: it was so hard that she broke a shovel trying to turn the soil over.

Yang had gardened long enough to recognize that two conditions had to be met: 1) she had to be patient, and 2) she had to get better soil. She immediately set up a composting area (eventually hidden in the back left corner by a "grove" of four birches).

While she was building better soil, she put her architectural design training to work. Given her small space, and all the garden themes she wanted to incorporate, Yang knew that she had to have the overall form worked out before she

Linda Yang has packed plants representing a life-time of garden friendships and a range of garden styles in her 18-foot-wide and 50-foot-deep Manhattan yard. Shown here is the herb garden, with her woodland glen in the background.

started planting.

The first decision was easy: eliminate the grass. It would only take maintenance time and crowd out other possible plants. Next, she studied the sunlight patterns falling on her property and picked the sunniest spot (about five hours in midsummer) for her herb garden.

Yang then proceeded to divide the garden into sections. To add interest, and to take away from the long hallway-like appearance of the yard, she decided to layer her approach; that is, soil was built up highest at the back and then dropped in a series of wide, steplike plateaus.

Each plateau forms a garden section in its own right. Trees were placed in the rear, where the soil was deepest; these also served to screen the property behind her. Rhododendrons and ferns complete the plantings in this section.

The herb garden was next. Here, Yang created a formal design bordered with bluestones. Flanking the square-shaped herb garden in the center are four right triangles, planted—depending on the light situation—with additional herbs or flowering shrubs. Roses climb the 6½-foot

wooden fence to the left, and a bench on the right invites one to sit and relish the scene.

From this area, the garden descends another level. Her husband dug out a walkway here to increase the contrast in garden levels. Two raised gardens fill up all space on each side of the depressed pathway. On the left, Yang has placed her 5-foot-long perennial border; on the right, a lotus pond and a moss garden are tucked in.

The garden ends—or begins, depending on one's point of view—at a bluestone terrace opening out from the back door. The vista is filled with hundreds of plants, with something in

LINDA YANG LIST OF EASY CARE SHADE FLOWERS

Lady's Mantle (*Alchemilla mollis*). Perennial with chartreuse flowers from late spring through early summer.

'Pumila' Astilbe (*A. chinensis* 'Pumila'). Perennial with raspberry pink flowers in summer.

Butterfly Shrub (*Buddleia davidii*). Shrub with purple flowers midsummer through fall.

Yellow Corydalis (*C. lutea*). Perennial with yellow flowers late spring through much, if not all, of summer.

Fringed Bleeding Heart (*Dicentra eximia*). Perennial with pink flowers late spring to fall.

Joe-Pye Weed (*Eupatorium purpureum*). Perennial with purple flowers late summer into fall.

Fuchsia (*F. x hybrida*). Annual (perennial in frost-free areas) with pink, purple, red, or white flowers through summer.

Kerria (*K. japonica* 'Pleniflora'). Shrub with yellow flowers late spring through early summer.

Big Blue Lobelia (*L. siphilitica*). Perennial with blue or white flowers late summer into fall.

Celandine Poppy (*Stylophorum diphyllum*). Perennial with yellow flowers spring through early summer.

Pink Foamflower (*Tiarella cordifolia* var. *wherryi*). Perennial with white or pale pink flowers in spring.

Wishbone Flower (*Torenia fournieri*). Annual with pink, purple, or white bicolor flowers early summer into fall.

Virginia Tovara (*T. virginianum* 'Variegata'). Perennial with cream-splashed green leaves and red flowers late summer to early fall.

bloom from February through October. The garden, however, is never the same from year to year as Yang continues to experiment, to try new flowers and herbs, to learn more about the possibilities of shade gardening.

Her mentors are now gone but memories of them are ever-present in the garden. When she searches for new information, she can almost feel the encouraging approval of Miss Hall; when she admires her long-blooming fringed bleeding heart, she is heeding Mrs. Morse's plea

to cultivate native plants; and when she cuts bright red roses for her black vase, she is following in her father's path.

FOR FURTHER INFORMATION on gardening in small spaces, see Linda Yang's *The City Gardener's Handbook: From Balcony to Backyard* (Random House, 1990, 318 pages). This tells not only about her experiences but also draws on interviews with small-space gardeners from coast to coast.

The Pumila astilbe is among the top easy care shade flowers named by Linda Yang. This summer blooming plant is also on the recommended flower lists submitted by the Boerner Botanical Gardens in Wisconsin and Marnie Flook in Maryland. It is pictured here in a July border created by David and John Jacobus in Princeton, New Jersey.

Photographed on May 10, Helen Benedict's flower beds in Rocky Hill, New Jersey, exhibit the colorful exuberance of the spring shade garden. Flowers pictured here include the foamy clumps of blue woodland phlox (primarily on the left), delicate sprays of forget-me-nots (center), and bright red, pink or white sieboldi primroses (right). Red-and-yellow flowers of American columbines dance in the background.

This section presents detailed descriptions of over 350 easy care shade flowering plants. There were actually many more to choose from. I wanted, however, only those that were most beautiful and easiest to grow. Initially my choice was limited by familiarity; that is, the plants were ones either I or my friends grew.

My list was further narrowed by the requirement that all plants had to be hardy in zones 4 to 8; i.e., in areas where winter lows vary from –30°F to +20°F. This means that they could be grown not only in Princeton but also in gardens from snowy Maine to sunny California, from frigid Michigan to balmy Alabama. To my core list, I added the superb shrubs honored by The Pennsylvania Horticultural Society's Gold Medal Award program and the plant recommendations provided by the gardeners profiled in Section II. And finally, I asked selected horticultural institutions across the country to recommend beautiful, environmentally friendly shade flowers for gardeners within their immediate areas.

Sixteen individuals or institutions compiled lists of easy care shade flowers for this book. It was extremely difficult for many to limit their choices, and a great deal of time and thought went into the recommendations. Over 100 plants were named. Only two—fringed bleeding heart and Virginia bluebells—are common to as many as five lists.

INSTITUTIONAL RECOMMENDATIONS

The following recommendations inadvertently illustrate the adaptability of shade flowers. San Francisco's Strybing Arboretum, for example, named the yellow-flowered Algerian epimedium, a spring-blooming plant that flourishes in the Princeton garden of my friend Mary Mills. One of my favorite fall bulbs, the colchicum, is on the Davis Arboretum's list of recommended dry shade plants for California's Central Valley. Though each institution lists plants suitable for its area, I think most readers will find superb shade flowers for gardens all over the country.

Here are the recommended plants provided by the various institutions, as well as brief descriptions of the organizations. All the flowers are available commercially in local areas. And all, with only three exceptions noted in the chapter descriptions, are offered by the mail order firms appearing in the Appendix. As is true of the lists presented in Section II, the first description of each plant indicates the chapter (Shrubs, Bulbs, etc.) in which a more detailed discussion appears.

CALIFORNIA

Davis Arboretum
University of California
Davis, CA 95616
(916) 752–4880

The Davis Arboretum of the University of California specializes in drought-tolerant plants adapted to the hot, dry summers and cool, wet winters of central California's Mediterranean-type climate. The Arboretum is known for its extensive collection of California native plants and its demonstration gardens of drought-tolerant flowering perennials. The following list of easy care, dry shade plants was submitted by arboretum superintendent Warren G. Roberts and nursery manager Ellen McEnroe Zagory. All of these plants are especially recommended for gardens in California's Central Valley; many can be grown throughout the country.

Western Redbud (*Cercis occidentalis*). Shrub with pink-purple flowers in late winter and early spring.

White Rockrose (*Cistus* x *hybridus*). Shrub with white flowers in summer.

Meadow Saffron (*Colchicum autumnale*). Corm

with white or light pink flowers in fall.

Showy Autumn Crocus (*Colchicum speciosum*). Corm with bright pink flowers in fall.

Baby Cyclamen (*C. hederifolium*). Tuber with pink or white flowers in fall.

Corsican Hellebore (*Helleborus lividus* subsp. *corsicus* but often listed or sold as *H. argutifolius*). Perennial with long-lasting green flowers that first open in early spring.

Island Alumroot (*Heuchera maxima*). Perennial with many tiny white flowers in spring.

'Santa Ana Cardinal' Coral Bells (*Heuchera maxima* x *H. sanguinea*). Perennial with rose red flowers spring through summer.

Candytuft (*Iberis sempervirens*). Perennial with abundant white flowers in spring and evergreen foliage.

Germander (*Teucrium chamaedrys*). Shrub with pink or white flowers in summer.

Bush Germander (*Teucrium fruticans*). Shrub with blue flowers in summer.

Strybing Arboretum and Botanical Gardens
Golden Gate Park
9th Avenue at Lincoln Way
San Francisco, CA 94122
(415) 661–1316

San Francisco's beautiful municipal botanical gardens reflect a successful public/private partnership. The city's Recreation and Park Department maintains the 70 acres of botanical gardens within Golden Gate Park and the nonprofit Strybing Arboretum Society provides educational programs. The following list of easy care, dry shade plants are among those recommended by Nursery Coordinator Don Mahoney in a spring 1991 article that he wrote for the Society's *Strybing Leaflet*. While all can be found in shade gardens throughout the San Francisco Bay area, they are also suitable for flower beds across the country.

Japanese Anemone (*A.* x *hybrida*). Perennial with white to many shades of pink flowers in fall.

European Columbine (*Aquilegia vulgaris*). Perennial with white, pink, purple, or blue flowers late spring into summer.

British Columbia Wild Ginger (*Asarum caudatum*). Groundcover with inconspicuous brown flowers in spring.

Foxglove (*Digitalis purpurea*). Biennial with white to deep pink flowers in late spring.

Algerian Epimedium (*E. perralderianum*). Perennial with yellow flowers in spring.

Bigroot Geranium (*G. macrorrhizum*). Perennial with magenta, rose, pink, or white flowers in spring.

Lenten Rose (*Helleborus orientalis*). Perennial with flowers in delicate white, pink, purple, or green tones in early spring.

Honesty (*Lunaria annua*). Biennial with purple or white flowers in spring and silvery white seedpods in fall.

Cineraria (*Senecio* x *hybridus*). Annual with white, red, blue, or purple flowers all summer.

ILLINOIS

The Lincoln Memorial Garden
Abraham Lincoln
Memorial Garden Foundation, Inc.
2301 East Lake Drive
Springfield, IL 62707
(217) 529–1111

A living memorial to Abraham Lincoln, the Garden's 77 acres along Lake Springfield's southern shore were designed by Jens Jensen. Wooden benches are strategically placed along the five miles of clearly marked nature trails. Only native Illinois plants are grown in the Garden. With the exception of a late fall application of Roundup on the Japanese honeysuckle (*Lonicera japonica*), no pesticides or fertilizers are used. The only Garden maintenance required is the weeding of nonnative plants such as periwinkle (*Vinca minor*) and the indomitable Japanese honeysuckle. The following list was submitted by Jim Matheis, the Garden's administrator.

American Columbine (*Aquilegia canadensis*). Perennial with red and yellow flowers in spring.

Marsh Marigold (*Caltha palustris*). Perennial with yellow flowers in early spring.

Tall Bellflower (*Campanula americana*). Annual with blue flowers in summer.

Dutchman's Breeches (*Dicentra cucullaria*). Perennial with white flowers in early spring.

Shooting Star (*Dodecatheon meadia*). Perennial with white to deep rose flowers in early spring.

White Snakeroot (*Eupatorium rugosum*). Perennial with white flowers late summer into fall.

Wild Geranium (*G. maculatum*). Perennial with blue-violet flowers in spring.

Round-lobed Hepatica (*H. americana*). Perennial with pale lilac to pinkish white flowers in early spring.

Virginia Bluebells (*Mertensia virginica*). Perennial with pink buds opening to sky-blue flowers in early spring.

Bloodroot (*Sanguinaria canadensis*). Perennial with white flowers in early spring.

Celandine Poppy (*Stylophorum diphyllum*). Perennial with yellow flowers spring through early summer.

MICHIGAN

Beal Botanical Garden
Michigan State University
East Lansing, MI 48824-1216
(517) 355–9582

The oldest continuously operating botanical garden in our country, the Beal Botanical Garden grows over 5,500 plant species and varieties. Many of these are displayed throughout Michigan State University's grounds. The Garden is both a teaching and a research facil-

ity. The following list was submitted by Gary B. Parrott, Grounds Manager at the University.

Marsh Marigold (*Caltha palustris*). Perennial with yellow flowers in early spring.

Winter Aconite (*Eranthis hyemalis*). Tuber with bright yellow flowers in late winter.

Arnold Promise Witch Hazel (*Hamamelis* x *intermedia* 'Arnold Promise'). Shrub with deep yellow flowers in late winter.

Virginia Bluebells (*Mertensia virginica*). Perennial with pink buds opening to sky-blue flowers in early spring.

Pokeweed (*Phytolacca americana*). Perennial with white flowers in summer and black–purple berries in fall.

Catawba Rhododendron (*R. catawbiense*). Shrub with lilac flowers in late spring.

Marie's Viburnum (*V. plicatum* var. *tomentosum* 'Mariesii'). Shrub with white clusters of flowers in late spring.

NORTH CAROLINA

North Carolina Botanical Garden
The University of North Carolina
at Chapel Hill
Campus Box 3375, Totten Center
Chapel Hill, NC 27599–3375
(919) 962–0522

The North Carolina Botanical Garden is a regional center for research on and conservation of plants, particularly those native to the southeastern United States, but also those horticultural plants with traditional uses or special botanical interest. Covering over 500 acres, the Garden is administered by the University of North Carolina at Chapel Hill and supported by the state of North Carolina and the Botanical Garden Foundation. The following list of shade tolerant plants is especially recommended for southern Piedmont gardens and was compiled by the Garden's staff.

American Columbine (*Aquilegia canadensis*). Perennial with red and yellow flowers in spring.

Jack-in-the-Pulpit (*Arisaema triphyllum*). Perennial with green-striped hooded flower in spring and bright red berries in late summer.

Canadian Wild Ginger (*Asarum canadense*). Groundcover with inconspicuous purplish brown flowers in spring and velvety heart-shaped green leaves throughout the growing season.

Goldenstar (*Chrysogonum virginianum*). Groundcover with yellow flowers spring, summer, and often into fall.

Fringed Bleeding Heart (*Dicentra eximia*). Perennial with pink flowers late spring to fall.

Cardinal Flower (*Lobelia cardinalis*). Perennial with scarlet red flowers in late summer.

Big Blue Lobelia (*L. siphilitica*). Perennial with blue or white flowers late summer into fall.

Beard Tongue (*Penstemon smallii*). Perennial with pink and white flowers in late spring.

Scorpionweed (*Phacelia bipinnatifida*). Biennial with lavender-blue flowers in spring.

The North Carolina Botanical Garden recommends the beautiful beard tongue as an easy care shade flower.

Blue Woodland Phlox (*P. divaricata*). Perennial with light blue flowers in spring.

Green Coneflower (*Rudbeckia laciniata*). Perennial with yellow flowers late summer into fall.

Bloodroot (*Sanguinaria canadensis*). Perennial with white flowers in early spring.

Fire Pink (*Silene virginica*). Perennial with red flowers in spring.

Pink Foamflower (*Tiarella cordifolia* var. *wherryi*). Perennial with white or pale pink flowers in spring.

O H I O

The Holden Arboretum
9500 Sperry Road
Mentor, OH 44060
(216) 946–4400

Harvard University's loss was Cleveland's gain at the beginning of this century when Albert Fairchild Holden decided to endow an arboretum in his home area rather than back east. Today, The Holden Arboretum is a unique 3,100-acre preserve containing over 6,800 plant species and cultivars in natural woodlands, horticultural collections, and display gardens. From its founding, the Arboretum's mission has been not only to collect, grow, and study flora, particularly that native to the midwestern region surrounding the Great Lakes, but also to promote the knowledge and appreciation of plants for personal enjoyment. The following list was submitted by Holden's Natural Areas Coordinator, Brian C. Parsons.

Doll's Eyes (*Actaea pachypoda*). Perennial with white flowers in late spring and distinctive white berries in fall.

Canadian Wild Ginger (*Asarum canadense*). Groundcover with inconspicuous purplish brown flowers in spring and velvety heart-shaped green leaves throughout the growing season.

Goldenstar (*Chrysogonum virginianum*). Groundcover with yellow flowers spring, summer, and often into fall.

Wintergreen (*Gaultheria procumbens*). Groundcover with white flowers in spring and bright red berries in fall.

Wild Geranium (*G. maculatum*). Perennial with blue-violet flowers in spring.

Crested Iris (*Iris cristata*). Perennial with light blue, lilac, purple, or white flowers in spring.

Twinleaf (*Jeffersonia diphylla*). Perennial with white flowers in spring.

Partridge Berry (*Mitchella repens*). Groundcover with pinkish white tubular flowers in summer and red berries in winter.

Miterwort (*Mitella diphylla*). Perennial with white flowers in spring.

Blue Woodland Phlox (*P. divaricata*). Perennial with light blue flowers in spring.

Creeping Phlox (*P. stolonifera*). Groundcover with purple-violet flowers in spring.

Celandine Poppy (*Stylophorum diphyllum*). Perennial with yellow flowers spring through early summer.

Allegheny Foamflower (*Tiarella cordifolia*). Groundcover with white flowers in spring.

WISCONSIN

Boerner Botanical Gardens
Whitnall Park
5879 South 92 Street
Hales Corners, WI 53130–2299
(414) 425–1131

Under the aegis of the Milwaukee County Park System, the internationally renowned Boerner Botanical Gardens include formal gardens designed by Alfred L. Boerner, test gardens for the All-American Rose Selections and the All-America Selections, and many specialty gardens. The following list of easy care shade flowers was compiled by staff members Ron Bahling, Julian Wesley, and Lori Yanny, and Director William J. Radler. The selections were based, Radler notes, on each plant having a long season of interest and being both hardy and resistant to drought and pests.

Goatsbeard (*Aruncus dioicus*). Perennial with creamy white flowers in late spring.

Kneiffii Goatsbeard (*Aruncus dioicus* 'Kneiffii'). Perennial with creamy white flowers in late spring.

Pumila Astilbe (*A. chinensis* 'Pumila'). Perennial with raspberry pink flowers in summer.

Fall Astilbe (*A. taguetti* 'Superba'). Perennial with lilac-pink flowers in late summer.

Black Cohosh (*Cimicifuga racemosa*). Perennial with candlelike spires of white flowers in summer.

Red Epimedium (*E.* x *rubrum*). Perennial with pink and yellow flowers in spring.

Yellow Archangel (*Galeobdolon luteum* but often listed and sold as *Lamiastrum galeobdolon*). Groundcover with yellow flowers in spring and green-and-silver foliage throughout the growing season.

Sweet Woodruff (*Galium odoratum* but also listed or sold as *Asperula odorata*). Groundcover with white flowers in spring.

Fall Hosta (*H. tardiflora*). Perennial with lavender flowers in fall.

Spotted Nettle (*Lamium maculatum*). Groundcover with purple ('Beacon Silver') or white ('White Nancy') flowers in spring, and green-and-silver foliage throughout the growing season.

European Jacob's Ladder (*Polemonium caeruleum*). Perennial with blue flowers in spring.

Lungwort (*Pulmonaria saccharata* 'Margery Fish'). Perennial with pink buds opening to blue flowers in spring and variegated green-and-gray foliage throughout the growing season.

P.J.M. Rhododendron (*R.* 'P.J.M.'). Shrub with lavender pink flowers in early spring.

Chapter Five

S H R U B S

Gold Medal Award winner Snow Queen hydrangea features sturdy cones of brilliant white flowers in early summer and crimson-to-wine red foliage in fall.

Shrubs constitute the heavy furniture in the shade garden room. There's nothing inconspicuous about them. While it is easy to overlook (and ultimately transplant or remove) unattractive bulbs or perennials, it is very hard to move shrubs.

Given that a diseased or inappropriate shrub can be so blatantly obvious, as well as difficult to get rid of, it is not surprising that most shade gardeners opt for a conservative approach and select plants such as rhododendrons and andromedas, which have proven track records. There are, however, many other beautiful, easy care shrubs that could add interest and a touch of the unusual to shaded settings.

GOLD MEDAL AWARD PROGRAM

Thanks to J. Franklin Styer, a nursery owner who initiated the Gold Medal Award Program of The Pennsylvania Horticultural Society (PHS), underutilized shrubs that are hardy, handsome, and low maintenance are now getting the attention they deserve. To qualify for a Gold Medal Award, a plant:

• must have reached landscape-size maturity in three separate botanical gardens, arboretums, or nurseries within 150 miles of Philadelphia, an area extending from Washington, D.C. to New York City (zones 5–8 for most plants); and

• must be available as stock for growers, retailers, and mail order sources.

Up to 14 ardent horticulturists serve on the award committee each year. They not only visit sites where each nominated plant is growing but also wade through all recommendation papers. The competition for a Gold Medal Award is keen; the arguments over which plants are worthy are sometimes heated; the results are always superior plants of exceptional merit

for the home gardener.

While Gold Medal Award winners are about evenly divided between sun- and shade-loving plants, the following selection describes only those that are suitable for shaded settings.

LAVENDER BEAUTYBERRY
Callicarpa dichotoma

This graceful plant needs to be placed in the sunniest position in your shade garden—preferably one that receives four to five hours of sun, and bright, open shade the remainder of the day. So situated, it will produce pink flowers on low, arching branches through most of July and August. The real bonus comes in September, when clusters of deep lilac fruits form; these look especially lovely in fall when all the leaves have fallen. Since the plant flowers and fruits on new wood, it can be pruned close to the ground in March or April, thus keeping its height at a compact 3 feet to 5 feet.

DAPHNE
D. caucasica

This plant is so ignored that it rarely appears in garden encyclopedias and has yet to earn a popular name. The PHS evaluators prized it highly for its delicately scented white flowers that bloom from April until frost. Its compact size (3 feet to 4 feet high) makes it a particularly valuable plant for north-facing front doors or patios. Like all daphnes, it needs good drainage.

SLENDER DEUTZIA
D. gracilis 'Nikko'

This compact, fine-textured shrub first came to the attention of the U.S. National Arboretum's John Creech and Sylvester March when they visited a Japanese nursery in 1976.

After 10 years, the Arboretum's original plant was 2 feet tall and had a spread of 5 feet. In the Philadelphia area, the shrub's abundant white flowers open in late May, and in fall the foliage turns a deep burgundy. This shrub is especially recommended for small gardens.

DWARF FOTHERGILLA
F. gardenii 'Blue Mist'

This beautiful plant, which has been described as providing "one of the most delightful displays of any flowering shrub," thrived in total obscurity at the Morris Arboretum of the University of Pennsylvania for over 50 years. No one knows how it arrived there. After observing its creamy white sprays of flowers every May, its blue-toned leaves through summer, and then its brilliant yellow foliage in the fall, horticulturists at the Arboretum decided to register this plant as a named selection in 1987. Since it reaches only 3 feet to 4 feet in height, it is perfect for small gardens or massed as a low hedge.

'DIANE' WITCH HAZEL
Hamamelis × intermedia 'Diane'

A hybrid between two Asian witch hazels, 'Diane' was originally promoted by the de Belders, Belgian nurserymen who specialize in exceptional witch hazels, and went on to win an Award of Merit from the Royal Horticultural Society in 1969. Often opening its large, deep red flowers in January, this 15-foot vase-shaped shrub also features brilliant red fall foliage. Needing winter sun, it looks especially grand and colorful when underplanted with white snowdrops or yellow winter aconites.

CHINESE WITCH HAZEL
Hamamelis mollis 'Pallida'

Steve Hutton, president of the Conard-Pyle

Larry Albee

Blue Mist dwarf fothergilla, shown here in a Philadelphia area garden, has puffs of white flowers in May, blue-toned leaves in summer, and brilliant yellow foliage in fall.

Company, was an enthusiastic nominator of this winter shrub featuring fragrant, lemon yellow flowers. It offers, he says, "a warm burst of color at a time of year when everything else, including people, is gray." At the University of Pennsylvania's Morris Arboretum, it begins to flower about the first of February and carries its blooms into mid-March. Growing up to 15 feet tall, this shrub needs space to be fully appreciated.

'DIANA' ROSE-OF-SHARON
Hibiscus syriacus 'Diana'

Those who know the long-blooming nature of the rose-of-Sharons also know that each flower sets seed and that that seed is very fertile. One of the glories of this cultivar, covered with large, lustrous white flowers that stay open so long each day that they often gleam in the moonlight, is that it is sterile. Other attributes, in addition to fabulous good looks, are that the plant can thrive along parking lots, in city gardens, and in formal gardens. Give it bright shade and four to five hours of direct sun. Left unpruned, it will grow 8 feet tall; pruned, it can form a neat 4-foot bushy hedge. This variety was created by the U.S. National Arboretum's Dr. Donald R. Egolf.

'BLUE BILLOW' HYDRANGEA

H. macrophylla subsp. *serrata* 'Blue Billow'

Dr. Richard W. Lighty found this plant in an open glade in Korea, while on a USDA plant exploration trip for Longwood Gardens in 1966. In 1982 he gave a plant to Winterthur Garden and the staff there thought it so beautiful that they began propagating it for commercial sales. This hydrangea features large quantities of intense blue lace-cap flowers that add drama to summer gardens. Since these bloom on year-old wood, it is best to prune shoots to the ground any time after flowering, from late summer to the following spring. This pruning also serves to keep the plant a neat and tidy 3-foot-to-4-foot rounded mound.

'SNOW QUEEN' OAKLEAF HYDRANGEA

H. quercifolia 'Snow Queen'

This southeastern U.S. native is such a beautiful, adaptable, and easy care plant that it should be found in gardens everywhere. Give it good soil, neither too wet nor bone-dry, and it will reach 5 feet to 6 feet at maturity, with an equal spread whether in full sun or full shade. It is prized for both its flowers and its foliage, which turns a lovely fall color—crimson to wine red, depending on the location. This Gold Medal Award winner was first selected by William Flemer III, president of Princeton Nurseries. It is drenched in upright cones of gorgeous white flowers in June and July; in addition to

being showier than those on the species plants, the 'Snow Queen' flowers are less likely to be shattered by summer thunderstorms. (See picture on page 65).

'HENRY'S GARNET' VIRGINIA SWEETSPIRE

Itea virginica 'Henry's Garnet'

Though inhabiting low, wet places in nature, this plant seems equally happy in garden soils that are dry. One of the first six plants to receive a Gold Medal Award, it was described as being "one of the finest shrubs to come along in a long time." Its fragrant white flowers appear in June and July, and its foliage turns a brilliant crimson in the fall. Hardier than the species, this cultivar was discovered growing in Georgia's woods in 1954 by Mary G. Henry and named for her, as well as for the color of its fall foliage. Another perfect shrub for small gardens, it reaches about 6 feet in height and 8 feet in breadth.

'ESKIMO' VIBURNUM

V. × 'Eskimo'

The U.S. National Arboretum has long had a breeding program which seeks to produce cultivars with superior ornamental beauty for nursery production and landscape use. Dr. Donald R. Egolf has been particularly successful in selecting shrubs for American home gardens. In first announcing news of this plant in 1981, he wrote that 'Eskimo' establishes a landmark in the development of elite Viburnum cultivars. It is compact (4 feet to 5 feet high), slow-growing, and has unusual, snowball-shaped flowers which in bud stage are pale cream with a touch of pink on the outer edge, and then open to pure white.

'WINTERTHUR' VIBURNUM

V. nudum 'Winterthur'

"All you have to do to covet [this plant] is to

see it on a crisp autumn morning with its mix of pink and dusty blue berries set against its rich purple foliage," wrote Dr. Richard Lighty, one of the 1991 Gold Medal Award evaluators. With a popular name of "possumhaw," it's hard to imagine this plant being an elegant addition to a garden, and yet it most certainly is. Discovered in 1961 in southern Delaware by the late Hal Bruce, curator of plants at Winterthur, this cultivar is shorter (6 feet) and more compact than the species while retaining all the virtues: large clusters of creamy white flowers in late spring, shiny dark green leaves throughout summer, and a memorable foliage and fruit display in fall.

DOUBLE FILE VIBURNUM
V. plicatum f. *tomentosum* 'Shasta'

Once again, gardeners can give thanks to the U.S. National Arboretum's Dr. Donald R. Egolf. In introducing this cultivar in 1979, he felt that it rivaled the dogwood in beauty. The lowest growing form of the double file viburnum, 'Shasta' is smothered in brilliant white flowers in late spring. It is twice as wide (12 feet) as it is high (6 feet). Birds love its red fruits; they are eaten so fast that they are rarely seen. The PHS recommends planting this shrub in a location from where its "milky way" display can be admired from above.

MORE EASY CARE SHADE SHRUBS

There are many other easy care, shade-flowering shrubs that gardeners might want to consider. Since most people have room for only a limited number of shade shrubs on their property (these plants, after all, do take up a lot of space), the following list has been kept deliberately short. All plants are recommended by one or more of the following: 1) gardeners or

institutions featured in this book, 2) the U.S. National Arboretum, and 3) me or my Princeton gardening friends.

While culture for these plants varies, most need to be planted in rich, organic soil that is well drained. The box on pruning (see page 71), gives some general tips on how to keep these shrubs looking neat and tidy. Mail order sources are listed at the end of the chapter.

GLOSSY ABELIA
A. × grandiflora

First grown in an Italian nursery sometime before 1880, glossy abelia languished in relative obscurity until it received an Award of Garden Merit from England's Royal Horticultural

Larry Albee

The Shasta doublefile viburnum, an introduction of the U.S. National Arboretum, is smothered by white flowers in May.

Society in 1962. That brought its long flowering period (through light frosts in my garden), shiny reddish green foliage, and ease of care to the attention of many. Recommended by the U.S. National Arboretum, this plant does best in light shade and well-drained soil. Pruning is required only for neatness in appearance.

Height: 5 feet
Color: White tinged with pink
Bloom Period: All summer into fall
Zones: 5–9

BUTTERFLY SHRUB
Buddleia davidii

A favorite of *New York Times* columnist Linda Yang, this shrub is generally recommended for full sun. Yang, however, successfully grows it in bright, open shade in a spot that receives about four hours of direct sun. This tough plant keeps on blooming until knocked out by frost; the more it is cut, the more flowers it produces. Naturalized in Europe, it was known for a long time as "Flower of the Ruins" after being found growing in the rubble of bombed-out buildings at Verdun. Butterflies, as the popular name indicates, love this plant. As far as maintenance goes, just prune it back to only 6 inches from the ground every spring and then sit back and enjoy its wonderful display.

Height: 20 feet
Color: White, lavender, dark purple
Bloom Period: Summer into fall
Zones: 6–9

CAROLINA ALLSPICE
Calycanthus floridus

Chiefly valued for the fruity fragrance of its flowers, this plant can take hefty doses of shade. Many garden books and articles recommend placing this shrub by a door so that its lovely aroma can easily be savored on warm summer evenings. Few bother to mention that Carolina allspice suckers and spreads; make sure you place it where it can be kept within bounds. The 'Edith Wilder' cultivar is exceptionally fragrant and has more abundant flowers.

Height: 4 feet to 9 feet
Color: Brownish maroon
Bloom Period: Spring
Zones: 4–9

REDBUD
Cercis

Small native trees, redbuds are spectacular in spring when their branches are covered with small, tightly packed purple-pink flowers. Here on the East Coast, they combine beautifully with white dogwoods; both bloom just as the soft green of woodland foliage begins to swell. In fall, redbud foliage turns a brilliant yellow.

Eastern Redbud (*C. canadensis*) This plant has a wide range, growing in light woodlands from New England to Florida. There are several cultivars, of which the U.S. National Arboretum recommends 'Forest Pansy', with purple foliage and white flowers; 'Silver Cloud', with variegated foliage; 'Wither's Pink Charm', with pink flowers; and 'Flame', with double flowers. The last was discovered growing wild near Fort Adams, Mississippi, in 1905; it is probably only marginally hardy in zone 5.

Height: 25 feet to 40 feet
Color: Purple, pink, white
Bloom Period: Spring
Zones: 4–9

Western Redbud (*C. occidentalis*) Native to California, this is smaller than Eastern Redbud and not as hardy. It is one of the dry shade

GENERAL GUIDELINES FOR PRUNING

Many shrubs, such as large rhododendrons and oakleaf hydrangeas, rarely need to be pruned. Others, however, do. Two basic reasons to prune a shrub are: 1) To removed diseased and dead branches, and 2) To control size and shape.

REMOVING DISEASED AND DEAD BRANCHES

Diseased branches should be removed as soon as they are noticed. This not only makes the plant look more attractive but also halts the spread of the disease. Dead branches can be cut at your convenience; the sooner the job is done, however, the more attractive the shrub.

CONTROLLING SIZE AND SHAPE

The timing of a shrub's flowering determines when it should be pruned for esthetic purposes. Basically, there are two shrub groups: those that flower in the spring on wood from the previous year and those that flower in summer on new wood.

GROUP ONE *Early Bloomers*
A sample of shrubs to prune in late spring or early summer

Azalea (*Rhododendron* species)
Carolina Allspice (*Calycanthus floridus*)
Slender Deutzia (*D. gracilis*)

Forsythia (*Forsythia*)
Kerria (*K. japonica*)

After spring flowers fade on these shrubs, the next year's buds form on new woody growth. By pruning immediately after flowering, you cut away old wood, and not the new growth with next year's buds.

Don't fret if there is no time to prune right after spring flowering. The shrub will just be bigger the following year. Large, unpruned forsythias, for example, look magnificent with their new, brightly flowered growth spraying over their interiors. If you feel a shrub is too big by the end of summer and decide to prune then, however, you are not harming the plant—you are just sacrificing some flowers in the coming spring.

GROUP 2 *Later Bloomers*
A sample of shrubs to prune in early spring.

Glossy Abelia (*A.* x *grandiflora*)
Butterfly Bush (*Buddleia davidii*)
Lavender Beautyberry (*Callicarpa dichotoma*)

Sweet Pepperbush (*Clethra alnifolia*)
Rose-of-Sharon (*Hibiscus syriacus*)

These shrubs all bloom on new wood; that is, the buds will form on growth beginning in spring. While these shrubs could be cut back in fall, the shorn limbs would be vulnerable to winter cold. The amount of cutting you do in early spring is determined by the size of shrub you want. Glossy abelia, for example, need never be pruned. As with the spring-blooming shrubs, you can always prune the plants later without harming them; you are just sacrificing some of the flower buds forming on the new stems.

plants recommended by the University of California's Davis Arboretum.

Height: 15 feet
Color: Pink-purple
Bloom Period: Late winter/early spring
Zones: 7/8–9

WHITE ROCKROSE
Cistus × *hybridus*

A bushy shrub, this bears large flowers in summer. It is recommended for dry shade gardens by the University of California's Davis Arboretum.

Height: 18 inches to 30 inches
Color: White
Bloom Period: Summer
Zones: 7–9

SWEET PEPPERBUSH
Clethra alnifolia

Recommended by the U.S. National Arboretum, this eastern native shrub is valued for its ease of maintenance and fragrant flowers, which bloom in midsummer. It is excellent for heavy shade and wet areas. This plant looks beautiful no matter where it's grown, both as an informal shrub in seashore gardens and as a clipped hedge in structured city garden settings. In the fall, the foliage turns a lovely yellow-orange.

Height: 6 feet to 8 feet
Color: White, pink
Bloom Period: Summer
Zones: 3–9

WINTERHAZEL
Corylopsis 'Winterthur'

Performing well in high shade, this lovely shrub has graced the grounds at Winterthur for over three decades. In late March its fragrant flowers begin to open. Densely clustered on numerous fine twigs, these form a beautiful announcement of the arrival of spring.

Height: 5 feet to 10 feet
Color: Pale yellow
Bloom Period: Early spring
Zones: 6–9

REDVEIN ENKIANTHUS
E. campanulatus

This old-fashioned shade shrub is treasured by plant connoisseurs and, for unknown reasons, largely ignored by gardeners. At the beginning of this century, L. H. Bailey deemed it "charming" and "handsome." In 1939, Harriet K. Morse recommended it for shade gardens. In 1984, George Schenk highly praised its elegance. Perhaps Allen Bush's glowing description in his 1992 Holbrook Farm catalogue will convince more gardeners to try this plant: "It does not have any serious disease or insect troubles, and it has attractive flowers and fall colors which beat all comers. The drooping, bell-shaped, creamy-yellow flowers tinged with red occur just before the leaves appear in mid-May. … In autumn the foliage turns shades of orange, red, and reddish-purple. I would argue that there are few shrubs to rival enkianthus for its complete ornamental value."

Height: 20 feet to 30 feet
Color: Flowers, cream or yellow with red veins; foliage, brilliant fall colors.
Bloom Period: Spring
Zones: 4–7

BURNING BUSH
Euonymus alata

The popular name for this shrub aptly describes its appearance in fall when its leaves turn a bright red. The more the shade, however, the less brilliant the color. This tough, undemanding shrub can be grown in any kind of soil.

Height: 9 feet to 12 feet
Color: Flowers, inconspicuous purple; foliage, bright red
Bloom Period: Spring
Zones: 3–8

FORSYTHIA
Forsythia

Insect- and disease-resistant, as well as capable of thriving in just about any soil, yellow-flowered forsythias are a familiar early spring shrub. Among the numerous species and hybrids, one stands out as being quite unusual and pretty: 'Winterthur' forsythia. This hybrid variety has pale yellow flowers that blend exquisitely, as can be seen at Winterthur Garden every spring, with the lovely yellows of 'Winterthur' witch hazel and the soft lavender of Korean rhododendron.

Height: 6 feet
Color: Pale yellow
Bloom Period: Early spring
Zones: 4–8

WITCH HAZEL
Hamamelis

Though good-looking, easy care, and featuring brilliant fall foliage, witch hazels are valued chiefly for their flowers, which open at a time when little else is in bloom. In addition to the two plants named below, two others have been honored by the Gold Medal Award program and are described in that part of this chapter.

'Arnold Promise' Witch Hazel *(H. × intermedia* 'Arnold Promise'*)* This hybrid is one of a series of crosses between Chinese (*H. mol-*

lis) and Japanese (*H. japonica*) species. Introduced by the Arnold Arboretum in Massachusetts, it bears larger flowers than most other witch hazels. These blossoms are a lovely yellow and cover the shrub in late February and early March. In the fall, the foliage turns a rich red and yellow.

Height: 20 feet
Color: Yellow
Bloom Period: Late winter
Zones: 5–8

Common Witch Hazel *(H. virginiana)* Native in moist, shady forests from Minnesota to Florida, this witch hazel blooms in fall; often the lovely yellow ribbonlike flowers will burst forth just as the last yellow leaf has fallen to the ground. The bark and leaves of this extremely easy care shrub were once used by Indians in tonics and teas to cure various ills, and its twigs were utilized as divining rods by early settlers.

Height: 12 feet to 15 feet
Color: Yellow
Bloom Period: Fall
Zones: 4–8

HYDRANGEA
Hydrangea

There are many species and cultivars of these beautiful, imposing shade garden shrubs. Two are described above under the Gold Medal Award program. The climbing hydrangea displays vine-like tendencies and is described in Chapter 6. Three other hydrangeas are described below.

Wild Hydrangea *(H. arborescens)* Recommended as a great seashore plant by the U.S. National Arboretum, this exceptionally easy care shrub is covered with cool white flowers during the height of summer heat. This is the first hydrangea introduced into Europe, its seed having been collected by American botanist John Bartram and sent to England just prior to the American Revolution. About a century later, the 'Grandiflora' cultivar was discovered growing in a gorge near Yellow Springs, Ohio. This has large flowers and, even more important to neat and tidy gardeners, is sterile—thus ensuring the absence of unwanted seedlings. 'Annabelle', yet another cultivar, has been introduced in recent years. A compact 4 feet, this is covered with 12-inch-wide white blossoms.

Height: 3 feet to 6 feet
Color: White
Bloom Period: Summer
Zones: 4–9

Garden Hydrangea (*H. macrophylla*) This old-fashioned plant comes in two forms: lace-caps and puffballs. I have the puffball version, which is known as Hortensia. Both will bloom with as little as three hours of direct sun; slightly more is even better. The color of the flowers is determined by the amount of aluminum in the soil; blue flowers result from high concentrations and pink flowers from little or no aluminum. Since the flowers bloom on the previous year's growth, never prune in spring.

Height: 3 feet to 6 feet
Color: Blue, pink
Bloom Period: Summer
Zones: 5/6–9

Peegee Hydrangea (*H. paniculata* 'Grandiflora') Though this plant is much too large for my property, I love seeing its large pyramidal clusters of late-summer flowers on sweeping shaded lawns in Princeton. *Wyman's Gardening Encyclopedia* says it is much too common a plant in American gardens. Once again, everyone has

his or her own opinion about plants. This hydrangea is one of the hardiest of the species.

Height: 20 feet to 30 feet
Color: Purplish pink
Bloom Period: Late summer into fall
Zones: 4–9

MOUNTAIN LAUREL
Kalmia latifolia

In the 1930s, according to *Wyman's Gardening Encyclopedia*, this native shrub was dug by the carload in the mid-south and shipped to northern gardens, where it is now a very common plant. Its fame spread across the country and it is now widely grown in California as well, particularly the 'Ostbo Red' cultivar.

Height: 7 feet to 8 feet
Color: White, pink
Bloom Period: Late spring
Zones: 4–9

KERRIA
K. japonica 'Pleniflora'

I tried and then discarded this shrub. In my small garden its orange-yellow flowers did not blend well with other plants; in addition, the kerria kept spreading and then, almost adding insult to injury, falling over other plants. Still, it will flower in quite a bit of shade and is recommended for dry places and city gardens by the U.S. National Arboretum. Linda Yang also rates it as one of her favorite easy care shade flowers.

Height: 4 feet to 6 feet
Color: Orange-yellow
Bloom Period: Spring, with sporadic repeat bloom
Zones: 5–8

OREGON GRAPE
Mahonia aquifolium

Native from British Columbia to northern California, this shrub can thrive in fairly heavy shade and is widely grown in western gardens. It has lacquered hollylike leaves, fragrant yellow flowers in spring, and clusters of plump blue berries. The last are edible and make a tart jam.

Though the Oregon grape is supposedly free of pests and diseases, I have seen some mighty sick—and deformed—plants in the Princeton area. Like the little girl with the curl on her forehead, when this is good it is very very good and when it is bad it is dreadful.

Height: 3 feet to 6 feet
Color: Flowers, yellow; berries, blue
Bloom Period: Spring
Zones: 4/5–8

The luscious pink and white flowers of the native mountain laurel are a favorite in outdoor gardens and indoor arrangements.

ANDROMEDA
Pieris

There are two popular garden species of this genus, one native from Virginia to Georgia and the other originally from Japan. Each requires four to five hours of direct sun to produce really lush displays of flowers. While both are handsome, spring-blooming plants, they are also, unfortunately, extremely susceptible to andromeda lacebug. This sucking insect produces up to three generations per garden year, each contributing hundreds of tiny pinholes on andromeda leaves, eventually causing many to brown and die. The result is not good-looking. For this reason, I have not tried this shrub. I have read, however, that the more shade it is given, the less the likelihood that it will be attacked by the andromeda lacebug.

Mountain Andromeda (*P. floribunda*) In stark contrast to the Japanese andromeda, which features drooping clusters of flowers, the native American mountain andromeda bears upright clusters of small white flowers. These almost blare forth the news of spring's arrival. When the andromeda lacebug is not around, the mountain andromeda is easier to grow than a rhododendron and can also take drought situations.

Height: 6 feet
Color: White
Bloom Period: Spring
Zones: 4–8

Japanese Andromeda, Lily-of-the-Valley Bush (*P. japonica*) *Wyman's Gardening Encyclopedia* proclaims this the nicest broad-leaved evergreen for planting in the north. Not quite as hardy as, and flowering earlier than, its native cousin, the Japanese andromeda has flowers resembling thick clusters of lily-of-the-valley.

Height: 9 feet
Color: White
Bloom Period: Spring
Zones: 5–8

RHODODENDRON
Rhododendron

This shade garden staple is described in greater detail in the profile of The Rhododendron Species Foundation in Chapter 3 (pages 36–39). In addition to the rhododendrons recommended by the Foundation, the following were also praised by others interviewed for this book. Five native rhododendrons—*R. arborescens*, *R. calendulaceum*, *R. maximum*, *R. periclymenoides*, and *R. prinophyllum*—were described as "outstanding ornamentals" on the list of easy care shade flowers submitted by Tom Stevenson, plant propagator at Bowman's Hill Wildflower Preserve.

All rhododendrons thrive in highly organic soil. Mulches—in the form of chopped leaves in fall and grass clippings in summer—serve to retain moisture, smother weeds, and provide an annual increase to the soil's organic matter.

Sweet Azalea (*R. arborescens*) Native from Pennsylvania to Georgia and Alabama, this shrub has been called the best hardy American white azalea. It features unusually fragrant white flowers, which have tiny reddish eyes, and foliage that turns a rich red in fall.

Height: 9 feet
Color: White
Bloom Period: Late spring
Zones: 4–9

Flame Azalea (*R. calendulaceum*) As its popular name implies, this shrub bears flame-colored flowers. Dubbed the showiest of native Americans, it can be found blooming for up to two spectacular weeks in woods from

Pennsylvania and Ohio to Georgia.

Height: 9 feet to 12 feet
Color: Orange, reddish orange, yellow
Bloom Period: Late spring
Zones: 5–8

Rosebay Rhododendron (*R. maximum*) An old-fashioned favorite, this is one of the hardiest of all rhododendrons; it survives in winters far away from its natural habitat bounded by North Carolina, Georgia, and Alabama. Its small flowers, nestling among evergreen foliage, appear later than those on most other rhododendrons.

Height: 12 feet to 36 feet
Color: Purple, rose pink, deep pink, white
Bloom Period: Early summer
Zones: 3–8

Snow Azalea (*R. mucronatum*) A very popular hardy azalea, this comes in several forms. 'Delaware Valley White', as its name implies, is drenched in white flowers. 'Winterthur', one of Henry Francis du Pont's favorite azaleas, has clear lavender blossoms that are as close to blue as any azalea's in existence. The flowers are also quite fragrant.

Height: 5 feet to 8 feet
Color: White, clear lavender
Bloom Period: Spring
Zones: 5–9

Korean Rhododendron (*R. mucronulatum*) Henry Francis du Pont achieved horticultural renown when he combined the pale lavender flowers of this shrub with the pale yellow of 'Winterthur' witch hazel and 'Winterthur' forsythia. Further north, Will Curtis was placing this same plant in a Garden in the Woods setting among brighter yellows and rich blues.

Obviously this lovely, easy care shrub looks handsome no matter where it is planted. Of note is that the flowers appear on bare branches and are then followed with rich green foliage that turns yellow to bronze-crimson in the fall.

Height: 6 feet
Color: Pale lavender
Bloom Period: Spring
Zones: 4–9

Pinxterbloom *(R. pericylmenoides)* Native from Maine to South Carolina and Tennessee, this tough, deciduous shrub bears lightly scented white to light pink flowers.

Height: 3 feet to 6 feet
Color: White to light pink
Bloom Period: Late spring
Zones: 3–8

'P.J.M.' Rhododendron *(R.'P.J.M.')* Bred by Weston Nurseries of Hopkinton, Massachusetts, and named for P. J. Mezitt, 'P.J.M.' rhododendrons are tough, beautiful hybrids that can take both frigid winters and hot summers. In late spring the plants are covered with rich lavender-pink flowers and in winter the foliage turns a mahogany color. This rhododendron is a favorite of the staff at Milwaukee's Boerner Botanical Gardens.

Height: 4 feet to 6 feet
Color: Lavender-pink
Bloom Period: Late spring
Zones: 4–8

Roseshell Azalea *(R. prinophyllum)* Another old-fashioned stalwart, this native shrub blooms through much of the U.S., appearing in woods from southern Quebec and Maine to southwest Virginia, west to Ohio and Illinois, and then south to Missouri, Arkansas, and Oklahoma. It has large fragrant pink flowers.

Height: 4 feet to 9 feet
Color: Pink
Bloom Period: Spring
Zones: 3–8

Plumleaf Azalea *(R. prunifolium)* The late Hal Bruce, curator of plants at Winterthur, considered this to be the most beautiful and unusual native azalea. I fell in love with this shrub when I saw its blazing red flowers gleaming by a trail at Garden in the Woods on a Labor Day weekend. What a surprise to read later that this native of Georgia and Alabama is supposed to bloom in July and is only hardy to zone 7! Thanks to Will Curtis's dedication to experimenting with many native plants, gardeners farther north of its natural habitat can plan with a reasonable hope of success to use this shrub as a beautiful late-season accent in their borders.

Height: 8 feet to 10 feet
Color: Flame red
Bloom Period: Depending on location, flowers open between early summer and Labor Day.
Zones: 5–8

(Pictured on page 30)

ROSE
Rosa

Here's what Daryl Johnson, rose curator at the International Rose Test Garden in Portland, Oregon, has to say about growing roses in shade: "If you can't get six hours of direct sunlight, plant something else." Some roses will bloom in shade, Johnson concedes, but they just pale in comparison with the splendors that can be obtained in a sunny setting.

Personally, I wouldn't grow roses even in full sun. In my experience, they are just not easy care plants. Insects such as Japanese beetles and aphids adore them and fungal diseases seem to be an integral part of their growth pattern.

Still, the number of rose lovers is great, and many of them have shade gardens. The following two roses have been recommended by friends as being exceptionally easy care and also good performers in shaded settings. Both are offered by Wayside Gardens (see address in Appendix).

'Betty Prior' is a long-blooming, old-fashioned floribunda rose. A rich pink in warm weather, the flowers turn progressively redder as temperatures cool. It reaches 4 feet to 5 feet in height and can be grown in zones 4–10.

'Gruss an Aachen' grows to the left of Liz Fillo's garage door in Princeton and is pictured on page 15. She bought the rose because it was claimed to bloom in semishade. "Guess it's true," she says, "since this doesn't get nearly the sun my other roses do and it blooms literally all summer with a dainty pink multipetaled flower, which is delicately scented." This rose can also be grown in zones 4–10.

FLOWERING RASPBERRY
Rubus odoratus

Native from Nova Scotia to Georgia, this shrub is valued for its long blooming period—all of July and August in my garden—and its ability to flower with less than one hour of direct sun. The flowers are a pinkish magenta and look lovely among the pale green leaves. There are no prickles.

In the dog days of late summer, the foliage will often be battle-weary from bouts with insects; I prune ruthlessly, and new greenery is produced just about the time the insects leave for richer pastures. This plant does spread.

Every spring, as I cut back the plant to 5 or 6 inches, I check for runners and rip them out.

Height: 9 feet (if left unpruned)
Color: Pinkish magenta
Bloom Period: All summer
Zones: 4–8

GERMANDER
Teucrium

The Davis Arboretum in California recommends both species below as being exceptional drought-tolerant plants for shaded situations.

Germander (*T. chamaedrys*) Often used in place of boxwood, this tough plant is also recommended by the U.S. National Arboretum as an evergreen shrub for edging or hedges. In addition to the good looks of its neat green foliage, it also produces pink or white flowers throughout summer.

Height: 1 foot to 2 feet
Color: White, pink
Bloom Period: Summer
Zones: 3–9

Bush Germander (*T. fruticans*) This evergreen shrub bears blue flowers throughout the summer months. Though available at local garden centers in California's Central Valley, it is not offered by major mail order nursery firms.

Height: 4 feet
Color: Blue
Bloom Period: Summer
Zones: 7–9

VIBURNUM
Viburnum

Viburnums are flowering shrubs highly

praised for their long season of interest. After being covered with beautiful blossoms in spring, these easy care plants sport richly textured summer foliage. In fall the plants offer a double bonus: brilliantly colored berries and reddish purple leaves. Three viburnums have received Gold Medal Awards and are described above. The following was recommended by Gary B. Parrott, grounds manager at Michigan State University in East Lansing.

Marie's Viburnum *(V. plicatum* var. *tomentosum* 'Mariesii'*)* Also recommended by the U.S. National Arboretum, this graceful shrub has sterile florets which are larger than the flowers on the species plant. Its red fruits mature to glistening black berries.

Height: 9 feet
Color: White
Bloom Period: Late spring
Zones: 4–8

In a bright shade setting that receives less than an hour of direct sun, the flowering raspberry (on the left) bears pinkish magenta flowers for over 2 months. It is pictured with the lavender flowers and dark green leaves of Hosta ventricosa *and the warm green leaves of* Hosta plantaginea.

SOURCES: The best place to buy shrubs is at a good local garden center or nursery, where you can purchase larger sizes than those obtainable through the mail. Most local establishments, however, do not offer the breadth of shrubs covered here.

With the exception of the rhododendrons, and unless noted in an individual description, all shrubs described above can be obtained from Forestfarm (see Appendix). While this firm's selection is extensive, the plants are all young—which means you must be patient before enjoying the mature aspects of their beauty.

In addition, the mail order firms of Bluestone Perennials, Crownsville Nursery, Holbrook Farm, and White Flower Farm offer limited shrub selections. Plants grown at Winterthur are sold at its Garden Shop and through its mail order catalogue. Many native rhododendrons are not offered commercially; check with The Rhododendron Species Foundation for information about obtaining these lovely plants.

As noted in the description of the Gold Medal Award program, winners must be commercially available. For further information about this program, or to obtain a copy of the retail and wholesale source list, send a stamped, self-addressed business-size envelope to the PHS Gold Medal Award, Pennsylvania Horticultural Society, 325 Walnut Street, Philadelphia, PA 19106.

Chapter Six

GROUNDCOVERS AND WALL CLIMBERS

Jean Woodward has managed to wall in the invasiveness of the green-and-white-foliaged goutweed. Other flowers crammed under a mountain laurel in her Princeton, New Jersey, garden include white spikes of foamflowers, yellow celandine poppies, blue American Jacob's ladders, and purple Beacon Silver spotted nettle.

Groundcovers and wall climbers are the carpets and curtains of the shade garden room, brightening up the earth below and the walls or trees above.

For the most part, the groundcovers in this chapter are valued either for their handsome mats of foliage or for their ability to cover areas in which few plants will thrive, areas such as spaces under shallow-rooted trees and shrubs. Since many of these groundcovers do well in "tough" spots, it only follows that they go berserk under ideal growing conditions. Caution should be exercised in introducing such plants to a garden border.

Many years ago, for example, I saw the green-and-white-foliaged goutweed in a friend's informal garden and asked for a clump. Upon being warned that it was invasive, I blithely replied that my clay soil was so thick nothing could spread too far.

For the first three years, all went well. In spring, the variegated foliage looked spectacular with the pink teardrops of the fringed bleeding heart; in summer, white flowers similar to Queen Anne's lace popped up; and in fall, the foliage provided a nice, bright look to a faded garden. Just to make sure the situation remained pleasurable, I would pull out shoots that had wandered beyond their assigned territory every fall during a general cleanup. By the fourth spring, however, the goutweed had taken off and was gleefully trampling over my flower border. Over the next two months, I spent many hours weeding it out.

My neighbor, Jean Woodward, took some of the plants, despite the cautionary advice from this now wiser gardener. Woodward learned from my experience, however. She placed the plant in a heavily shaded location under a mountain laurel, an area where she did not have a formal garden and where she wanted color without maintenance. She combined the goutweed with other tough shade plants: spotted nettle, Allegheny foamflower, American Jacob's ladder, lungwort, fringed bleeding heart, and celandine poppy. Then she stepped back and let them fight out their own turf wars.

Five years later, as shown in the picture on the left, Woodward can proudly point to a most successful planting ploy. In the spring, this area is filled with pink, blue, and yellow flowers. For the remainder of the growing season, the foliage contrasts—particularly highlighted by the green-and-white of the goutweed—look handsome in a dark setting. In addition, Woodward usually enlivens the scene by tucking in a few colorful impatiens. These are placed in front of the border, and when she is planting them, she pulls out any goutweed that has wandered that far. (Author's Note: I still think the goutweed will eventually win out.)

With regard to wall climbers, *The New York Times*'s Allen Lacy recently wrote that vines may be the next trend in gardening. He feels these plants not only add a vertical dimension to the garden but also impart a sense of aspiration.

My flower borders shall not be part of any such trend. For almost twenty years I have gardened next to a property in which Japanese honeysuckle is rampant; it wants nothing better to do than to extend its conquest into my property. I have spent more hours hacking away at that vine than I have in attacking any weed on my own grounds. Though it is probably unfair to the vines described below (all recommended by other gardeners), I just can't bring myself to introduce one on my property.

Of course, there are additional wall climbers besides vines. Many require a fence or a trellis for support, and I don't feel like putting in that much effort. Should I feel so inclined, however, I would definitely want to try the 'Betty Corning' clematis (recently honored with a Gold Medal Award by The Pennsylvania Horticultural Society) and the hardy fuchsia. The first has beautiful blue flowers that open through most of the summer, and the second has gorgeous, drooping scarlet blossoms that do bloom all summer.

Frederick and Mary Ann McGourty, owners of beautiful Hillside Gardens Nursery in Norfolk, Connecticut, have stunningly demonstrated the heights to which a climbing hydrangea can go (see picture on page 18). Had I a similarly tall tree for this plant to grow on, I would most certainly try to emulate their example.

If you would like a groundcover or a wall climber in your shade garden, consider one or more of the following. Unless noted otherwise under an individual description, the installation and maintenance of these plants are quite simple. Give them the kind of soil they like, cover their roots, and then leave them on their own (many of the climbers, of course, must be tied). Mail order sources are presented at the end of the chapter.

EASY CARE SHADE GROUNDCOVERS

GOUTWEED

Aegopodium podagraria 'Variegatum'

This is not only invasive but also extremely difficult to weed out. It is certainly worth considering, however, for places with dry, dark, poor soil where a bright bit of striking green-and-white foliage would perk up the setting.

Height: 6 inches to 14 inches
Color: Flowers, white; foliage, green-and-white
Bloom Period: Late spring
Zones: 3–9
  (Pictured on page 80)

BUGLEWEED

Ajuga reptans

I originally tried to use this as a border plant. Within two years it had marched away from the flower bed and spread throughout the lawn. This is a plant that takes to grass the way a duck takes to water. In a controlled setting—an area where boundaries are strictly defined either by rocks, bricks, or metal underground edging material—bugleweed is a great easy care shade plant. It has little spikes of blue flowers in the spring and a rich green foliage mat the rest of the growing season. New cultivars have been developed with white or pink flowers and with lovely multicolored foliage; most gardeners think them far superior to the species plant.

Height: 4 inches to 8 inches
Color: Flowers, blue or white; foliage, green, bronze, white, pink, or multicolored
Bloom Period: Spring
Zones: 3–9
  (Pictured on page 123)

WILD GINGER

Asarum

Low-growing and thriving in the dappled light of deciduous woods, wild gingers add a touch of class to shade gardens. All are grown chiefly for the elegance of their foliage, with leaf size, texture, and coloration varying among the species. As woodland plants, wild gingers need slightly acidic soil that is rich in organic matter. The easiest way to increase their numbers is through division in spring or, preferably, fall.

Canadian Wild Ginger (*A. canadense*) Native from Canada to Alabama and from South Carolina to Kansas, this is probably the easiest species to grow in American gardens outside the Pacific Coast area. It spreads slowly by rhizomes (which have been used as a culinary ginger substitute) and has lovely heart-shaped leaves.

Height: 6 inches to 10 inches
Color: Flowers, purplish brown; foliage, velvety green
Bloom Period: Spring
Zones: 4–8

British Columbia Wild Ginger (*A. caudatum*) This handsome Pacific Coast native features kidney-shaped leaves. It is recommended by the U.S. National Arboretum as well as by San Francisco's Strybing Arboretum nursery coordinator Don Mahoney, who says it is particularly suitable for dry shade gardens.

Height: 7 inches to 9 inches
Color: Flowers, brown; foliage, velvety green
Bloom Period: Spring
Zones: 4–9

European Wild Ginger (*A. europaeum*) The sumptuously rich heart-shaped leaves on this plant glisten in gardens and provide a further treat by remaining evergreen in most areas. This wild ginger is also recommended by the U.S. National Arboretum.

Height: 5 inches to 8 inches
Color: Flowers, dull brown; foliage, glossy green
Bloom Period: Spring
Zones: 4–8

PLUMBAGO
Ceratostigma plumbaginoides

Supposedly an easy to grow, somewhat invasive plant, plumbago has yet to thrive on my property. Part of the problem could be that I have placed it in rather dry areas. And though I have yet to come across anyone who has had insect problems with this plant, there is something that loves to nibble mine to pieces. Those bright shade gardeners who are successful with plumbago are rewarded with deep blue flowers in summer and lovely bronze-red foliage in the fall; some are lucky enough to have the two colors overlap.

Height: 8 inches to 12 inches
Color: Blue
Bloom Period: Summer into fall
Zones: 5–10

GOLDENSTAR, GREEN-AND-GOLD
Chrysogonum virginianum

Native to the eastern U.S., this colorful woodland groundcover needs moist, rich, humusy soil. I think the brightness of its yellow has kept me from acquiring it; somehow it seems too rich among the pale pinks and many blues of my spring borders. And yet, goldenstar is so highly praised by horticulturists I respect—Allan M. Armitage, Ruth Clausen, Frederick McGourty—that I feel I really should have it in my borders. If it survives slug damage, visitors will soon find it adorning a brightly shaded area in one of my gardens.

Height: 4 inches to 10 inches
Color: Yellow
Bloom Period: Spring to fall in cooler areas, spring to early summer in warmer ones
Zones: 5–10
(Pictured on page 43)

BUNCHBERRY
Cornus canadensis

This is a diminutive relative of our native dogwood trees. It bears good-looking green foliage and flowers and fruit very similar to that on its taller relatives. I had never heard of it until doing the research for this book. Its natural range—woodlands in Greenland and Labrador to Alaska and east Asia, south to West Virginia, New Mexico, and California—suggests that it is very adaptable to different climate situations. Most garden books, however, say it requires cool, moist growing conditions.

Height: 9 inches
Color: Flowers, white; berries, red
Bloom Period: Spring
Zones: 2–7

YELLOW ARCHANGEL

Recently classified as *Galeobdolon luteum,* this is generally listed and sold as *Lamiastrum galeobdolon*

This is a groundcover for dry, dark—or even moist, dark—places where it seems nothing will grow. Put it in more hospitable situations, and it will rapidly take over. In my zone 6 garden, the foliage is often scarred by winter cold. Still, there always seems to be enough to pick a sprig or two in late January or early February when I am desperate for some outside activity in the garden. In the spring, lots of new green-and-silver foliage appears, to be shortly followed by

spikes of yellow flowers that last up to three weeks. In one very dark corner the plants do not flower at all, but the lovely variegated foliage does quite well.

Obviously, I like this plant. Most other garden experts, however, prefer one of two cultivars: 'Herman's Pride', which is less aggressive and has smaller flowers and leaves, or 'Variegatum', which has leaves that are basically white with small green markings.

Height: 9 inches to 20 inches
Color: Flower, yellow; foliage, green-
        and-silver
Bloom Period: Spring
Zones: 3–9

SWEET WOODRUFF

Galium odoratum; also listed and sold as
Asperula odorata

This is a lovely plant, with snow-white flowers in spring and warm green foliage. The crushed leaves flavor May wine; in Victorian times, they were also used in sachets as a moth repellent. The attractiveness of this dainty groundcover is best seen when it is placed under woody shrubs, such as rhododendrons and sweetspires.

Height: 4 inches to 10 inches
Color: White
Bloom Period: Spring
Zones: 3–9

Blue Spanish squills pop up among the white flowers of sweet woodruff in one of Liz Fillo's mid-May beds in Princeton, New Jersey. See page 25 for a picture of this setting two months later.

WINTERGREEN
Gaultheria procumbens

In recommending this plant for American gardens, the U.S. National Arboretum classified it as an historic herb, since the berries and leaves from this plant were used by Indians to make medicinal teas. While some eat the berries to this day (the taste is supposed to be refreshing), most grow this groundcover for the beauty of its evergreen leaves and its tiny but pretty white bell-like flowers.

Height: 3 inches to 6 inches
Color: Flowers, white; berries, red
Bloom Period: Spring
Zones: 4–8

CHAMELEON PLANT
Houttuynia cordata 'Variegata'
('Chameleon')

There are mixed reactions to this groundcover. Some of my garden friends despise it for its invasiveness, and others laud it for the attractiveness of its multicolored foliage in shady nooks. If you decide to try it, be wary of the former and remember that the darker the location, the less red or yellow coloring on the foliage.

Height: 6 inches to 24 inches
Color: Flowers, white; foliage, green splashed with cream, pink, and red
Bloom Period: Summer
Zones: 5–9

SPOTTED NETTLE
Lamium maculatum

To me, the cultivars of this plant (the species is rarely grown) appear to be dainty, refined versions of the yellow archangel. Since I have the latter, I don't feel the need to obtain the former. Most of my garden friends do grow these plants, however, particularly the 'Beacon Silver' and the 'White Nancy' cultivars. Both have pretty flowers (the first purple and the second white) and lovely silver foliage edged with green. 'White Nancy' is more disease-resistant than 'Beacon Silver.'

Height: 6 inches to 14 inches
Color: White, pinkish purple, reddish purple
Bloom Period: Spring, sporadically through summer
Zones: 3–10
(Pictured on pages 80 and 86)

LILYTURF
Liriope

Plants in this genus are neat, good-looking, and grow in just about every kind of shade setting. Their foliage resembles that of grass and their flowers those of an elongated grape hyacinth. They are valued for their ease of care, their late summer bloom, and their ability to do well in dry shade. In fact, the last is an ideal situation in which to place these plants as moister soils often harbor slugs, and these creatures view lilyturf as a real taste treat.

Big Blue Lilyturf (*L. muscari;* sometimes listed and sold as *L. platyphylla*.) This is a wonderful plant for southern gardens, particularly those in hot and humid areas such as Florida. Of the many cultivars, the U.S. National Arboretum recommends two: 'Variegata' and 'Christmas Tree'.

Height: 12 inches to 24 inches
Color: Purple
Bloom Period: Late summer into fall
Zones: 6–10

Creeping Lilyturf (*L. spicata*) This lilyturf spreads faster than big blue lilyturf and can

Big blue lilyturf, photographed in late August at the Visitors Center at the U.S. National Arboretum in Washington, D.C., is perfect for dry shade areas.

Color: Flowers, yellow; foliage, greenish yellow
Bloom Period: Early summer
Zones: 3–8

MAZUS
M. reptans

The first time I tried to grow this really pretty groundcover, I placed it in an extremely dry situation: a bare dirt area where even weeds were having a hard time settling in. The poor plant wilted away. The second time, I put it in a bright shade area where bugleweed, crab grass, and moss thrive. The mazus took off, shoving aside the moss in particular. It forms a soft green carpet—one that is walked on sporadically—for most of the year and a beautiful display of flowers throughout the month of May.

withstand colder temperatures. Its flowers, however, are smaller and not as showy. Still, northern gardeners who are away much of the summer, or who are too busy to pay much attention to their flower beds, will find this plant a spreading, reliable bloomer.

Height: 8 inches to 14 inches
Color: Lavender
Bloom Period: Late summer into fall
Zones: 4–10

YELLOW CREEPING JENNY
Lysimachia nummularia 'Aurea'

This plant is grown for its foliage, which looks like a spreading mat of greenish yellow coins. A European native, it can now be found growing wild in woodland areas in the U.S. where the soil is moist. In the garden, care should be taken to make sure its bold color complements that of other plants placed with it.

Height: 4 inches to 8 inches

Carol Rothberg has allowed the purple flowers of Mazus reptans to wander about a shaded back walk at her Princeton, New Jersey, home. To the left, variegated clumps of White Nancy spotted nettle and light blue sprays of forget-me-nots add further color to this mid-May picture.

This is a wonderful groundcover for filling in areas around stepping-stones.

Height: 1 inch to 2 inches
Color: Purple-blue spotted with white and yellow
Bloom Period: Spring
Zones: 5–9

PARTRIDGE BERRY
Mitchella repens

A native American, this plant cuts a wide swath, growing under trees from Nova Scotia to Ontario and Minnesota and south to Florida, Texas, and eastern Mexico. It is truly a plant for all seasons: evergreen foliage with whitish veins in spring, pretty tubular flowers in summer, bright red berries in fall, and a wonderful Christmas decoration in winter. Even if you don't grow this plant, you will often see it in florist's arrangements or in dining-table centerpieces over the holidays. Heather McCargo, plant propagator at Garden in the Woods, highly recommends it for its ease of care and good looks.

Height: 6 inches to 12 inches
Color: Flowers, pinkish white; berries, red
Bloom Period: Summer
Zones: 3–9

PACHYSANDRA
Pachysandra

One can see evergreen carpets of Japanese pachysandra throughout the Northeast and, frankly, I think they are boring. Still, except for an occasional fungus attack, the plant is an easy care, useful shade groundcover. Our native Allegheny pachysandra has prettier flowers and is more interesting than the ubiquitous Japanese pachysandra. As indicated in the climate zone data, it is also more suitable for warmer areas.

Allegheny Pachysandra (*P. procumbens*)

Height: 6 inches to 12 inches
Color: White to purple
Bloom Period: Spring
Zones: 4–9

Japanese Pachysandra (*P. terminalis*)

Height: 6 inches to 12 inches
Color: White
Bloom Period: Spring
Zones: 3–8

CREEPING PHLOX
P. stolonifera

In recognition of creeping phlox's beauty and ease of care, The Perennial Plant Association named it flower of the year in 1990. This plant takes heavy shade, is covered with flowers in late spring, and forms a thick evergreen mat. Though creeping phlox has purple-violet flowers in its native Appalachian Mountains, new cultivars have been developed with white, blue, or pink blossoms.

Height: 6 inches to 12 inches
Color: Purple-violet, blue, pink, white
Bloom Period: Spring
Zones: 3–9

MAYAPPLE
Podophyllum peltatum

If I had a large woodland garden, this plant would definitely be included. In early spring it pushes aside leafy accumulations and sends up green umbrellalike foliage atop an erect stem. The upper leaves float throughout the woods as if a major fairy convention were being held during the rainy season. Several weeks later, those who care to peek below the umbrella will see pretty white flowers tucked inside. Greg Edinger, museum educator at Bowman's Hill

Wildflower Preserve, rates this as one of his favorite easy care shade flowers.

Height: 18 inches
Color: White
Bloom Period: Spring
Zones: 3–9

GOLD MOSS
Sedum acre

This is usually described as a rock garden plant, a good creeper that fills in nooks and crannies in full sun and with some moisture. I hadn't read these descriptions when I stuck some in a narrow border by the northern corner of my house; while little sun touches down here, there is bright light reflected from our white aluminum siding. The gold moss filled up the space not covered by the yellow flag iris. While I can't take credit for any prior planning, I do delight in the scene when these two plants bloom at the same time—the effect is quite lovely. The rest of the season, the arching foliage sprays of the iris nicely complement the underlying warm green leaves of the gold moss.

Height: 2 inches to 3 inches
Color: Yellow
Bloom Period: Spring
Zones: 3–9

ALLEGHENY FOAMFLOWER
Tiarella cordifolia

The Primrose Path catalogue endorses this plant with high praise: "In our opinion, this is the finest and easiest native groundcover for shade, succeeding even in fairly dense shade under evergreens." In a woodland setting, the Allegheny foamflower can be invasive, spreading quickly by stolons to carpet a forest floor. Therefore, some care should be taken in plac-

ing it in a smaller setting. In diminutive borders, the pink foamflower might be more suitable; it does not spread, increasing slowly as a clump (see its description in Chapter 10). Gardeners with large areas to cover, however, will be more than satisfied with the Allegheny foamflower, particularly in spring when its foamy spikes of white flowers splash through the woods.

Height: 6 inches to 12 inches
Color: White
Bloom Period: Spring
Zones: 3–9
    (Pictured on page 80)

PERIWINKLE
Vinca minor

An escaped major pest in some woodland gardens, periwinkle is an easy care gardener's joy in others. Its dark green leaves are evergreen and its blue flowers are lovely in spring. I originally placed some in a garden border—big mistake—and am still weeding it out. Some of these "weeds" were transplanted to a dry, shaded area underneath a fir tree and interplanted with ivy—great success. The two groundcovers fight for space and, after five years, neither one has taken over. Meanwhile, few weeds are able to nestle in, and the area looks presentable throughout the year.

Though I do not grow them, there are two periwinkle cultivars that are generally recommended. These are 'Alba', which has white flowers, and 'Variegata', which has variegated leaves. Both are excellent container plants.

Height: 3 inches to 6 inches
Color: Blue, white
Bloom Period: Spring
Zones: 5–9
    (Foliage pictured on page 46)

VIOLET
Viola

Violets are the perennial versions of the garden pansy. The many different species of this genus bear flowers in a variety of colors, including white, yellow, purple, and blue. When not bothered by pests, these are charming plants for the spring border. I have tried several varieties and have had disastrous results, because the same conditions under which the plants thrive—shady, moist soil—are also those under which slugs replicate freely. I planted the repeat-blooming yellow violet (*V. pensylvanica*) one afternoon and couldn't believe that it had totally disappeared by the next morning. Slug trails—slimy tracks that glisten in light—left an obvious clue. While I have had success with the following two plants, this may be due to the fact that the slugs have yet to zero in on them.

Appalachian Violet (*V. appalachiensis*) With its small, dainty foliage and restrained spreading habit, this is a very refined violet. In some ways it looks like a miniature wild ginger. Unlike the asarums, however, this plant has pretty flowers—small purple blossoms that appear for over four weeks in my garden. Given its ground-hugging tendency and its mat-forming way of spreading, I think this would be a perfect groundcover for gardens on slopes. Rarely offered commercially, plants can be obtained from The Wildwood Flower.

Height: 1 inch to 2 inches
Color: Violet
Bloom Period: Spring
Zones: 5–8

Labrador Violet (*V. labradorica* var. *purpurea;* also listed as *V. riviana purpurea.*) Its short stature and purple-tinged foliage make this an excellent and attractive groundcover. It spreads by slender, creeping rhizomes; once settled in, these can become invasive.

Height: 1 inch to 4 inches
Color: Flower, purple; foliage, purple-tinged
Bloom Period: Spring
Zones: 3–8

EASY CARE SHADE VINES AND OTHER WALL CLIMBERS

CLEMATIS
Clematis

Hundreds of species and cultivars of this plant adorn gardens both here and in Europe, particularly in Great Britain. The English often train these plants to climb about stately, pyramid-shaped green firs; the result is spectacular. In my Princeton, New Jersey, neighborhood, several gardeners have enhanced the attractiveness of the street scene by planting clematis vines at the base of the township's "No Parking" signs. The vines crawl up rather ugly steel rods, cover them profusely, and bloom most of the summer.

While clematis vines do well in bright or part shade, they must be planted in soil that is not overly acidic and that keeps their roots cool and moist. The following three are exceptionally hardy and easy care. All bloom on new wood; thus, if you wish to restrain their size, cut them back in early spring before growth starts.

Jackman Clematis (*C. × jackmanii*) Created in 1858 by the English nursery firm of George Jackman and Sons, this was the first large-flowered hybrid and the originator of a breeding program that continues to this day. There are many cultivars that come and go according to popular fancy. Just look for a version of the name "Jackman" and you should be rewarded with a plant with beautiful blooms 4 inches to 7 inches across.

Height: 12 feet
Color: Purplish violet
Bloom Period: Summer to frost
Zones: 3–8

Sweet Autumn Clematis *(C. maximowicziana;* also listed and sold as *C. paniculata.) Wyman's Gardening Encyclopedia* states that this is one of the most dependable; a glance in late summer at the railroad tracks between New York and Philadelphia demonstrates quite vividly how true that statement is. It climbs about banks filled with civilization's ugly discards and rambles up guy wires, covering all with a profusion of late August and early September white flowers. In this wild, naturalized setting, the plant is never pruned. In a home garden, a yearly cutback in early spring should make it a well-behaved member of a flower border receiving four to five hours of sun.

Height: 30 feet
Color: White
Bloom Period: Late summer into fall
Zones: 4–9

'Betty Corning' Clematis *(C. viticella* 'Betty Corning') A recent recipient of The Pennsylvania Horticultural Society's Gold Medal Award, 'Betty Corning' was described by a PHS evaluator as follows: "This plant is remarkable for the profusion of blossoms starting in June. Mine is growing on a north-facing wall under a 33-foot roof overhang. It blooms heavily in this dark and often dry location." The plant is named for its discoverer, who found it growing on a porch on an Albany, New York, side street in 1933. Mrs. Corning asked for, and received, a cutting of this plant. And just in time, too, for soon afterward the house with the mother plant was demolished.

Height: 6 feet to 10 feet

Color: Silver on the outside, lavender-blue on the inside
Bloom Period: Late spring through July, and often a repeat bloom after Labor Day
Zones: 4–8

HARDY FUCHSIA
F. magellanica

A native of Peru and Chile, this long-flowering shrub is now naturalized along roadsides in southern Ireland. It has also done well farther north in its home hemisphere; the U.S. National Arboretum highly recommends it. Best viewed when trained on a wall or trellis, hardy fuchsia needs to be cut back almost to the ground in early spring.

Height: 12 feet
Color: Red
Bloom Period: All summer to frost
Zones: 4/5–8

Judy Jakobsen

The red flowers of a hardy fuchsia glow in an October garden on California's Mendocino coast.

CLIMBING HYDRANGEA

H. anomala subsp. *petiolaris*

As mentioned earlier, Frederick and Mary Ann McGourty's garden in Norfolk, Connecticut, displays this plant in all its glory. It climbs majestically on an ash tree, entwining the trunk with white flowers. This grand plant, however, needs a grand setting, and so it is not for all shade gardeners.

Height: 75 feet
Color: White
Bloom Period: Late spring to early summer
Zones: 4–7
(Pictured on page 18)

HONEYSUCKLE

Lonicera

Though my encounters with the invasive Japanese honeysuckle have given me an intense dislike for this genus, other gardeners feel the following are beautiful, easy care, and not terribly invasive.

Goldflame Honeysuckle *(L. × heckrottii)* Recommended by the U.S. National Arboretum as being the most beautiful and fragrant of the honeysuckles, this vine is a mutt of unknown origin. Though it acquired its botanical name in the early part of this century, it languished in obscurity until a Kansas nurseryman dubbed the plant "goldflame." With such a catchy, and accurate, description of its long-blooming flowers, the plant took off and has been seen in gardens across the country ever since.

Height: 12 feet to 20 feet
Color: Carmine, opening to yellow, and then changing to pink

Bloom Period: Late spring through early frosts
Zones: 4–8
(Pictured on page 15)

Woodbine *(L. periclymenum)* Recommended by the U.S. National Arboretum as well as by British garden expert Anna Scott-James, this vine and its cultivars are good choices for smaller gardens. As pictured on page 15, Liz Fillo beautifully paired a cultivar of this plant, 'Graham Thomas', with the goldflame honeysuckle. The cultivar is named for the renowned English horticulturist Graham Stuart Thomas, who serendipitously discovered it growing in a Warwickshire hedgerow.

Height: 8 feet
Color: Yellow-white
Bloom Period: Summer to frost
Zones: 5–9

Trumpet Honeysuckle *(L. sempervirens)* This American native grows on its own from Connecticut to Florida, west to Texas; it is recommended by the U.S. National Arboretum. Covered with colorful flowers in summer, it also features long-lasting fruits that attract many birds, including hummingbirds.

Height: 12 feet to 20 feet
Color: Red, orange, yellow
Bloom Period: All summer
Zones: 4–8

SOURCES: Each plant in this chapter is offered by one or more of the following mail order nurseries: Bluestone Perennials, Crownsville Nursery, Forestfarm, Primrose Path, and White Flower Farm. Addresses for these firms are in the Appendix.

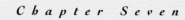

Chapter Seven

BULBS, CORMS, AND TUBERS

A torrent of white-flowered ramsons cascade through a woodland in Cornwall, England. As shown, English bluebells are pushed aside by the aggressive ramsons.

With their bright colors and striking flowers, bulbs are wonderful additions to gardens in shaded settings. From late winter, when the shining yellow of winter aconite brightens cold brown patches of bare earth, through the first blasts of fall frost, when the delicate pinks of autumn crocuses freshen up late season gardens, bulbs are the epitome of easy care flowers.

In general, spring- and fall-flowering bulbs are hardy; that is, they require a period of dormancy and cold weather before setting out new blossoms. They also tend to be short, usually growing no more than 1 foot in height.

Summer bulbs tend to be taller, some reaching 6 feet. And, with the notable exception of alliums and lilies, they are usually tender; that is, they cannot withstand freezing temperatures and, if not taken out of the ground for safekeeping over the winter months, will only last one year in the garden. This, to my way of thinking, is not easy care. Thus I have included only four tender bulbs, chosen either for their dramatic appearance, long flowering time, or recommendation by others. In purchasing just one or two pots of these plants, you can discard them at the end of the growing season—or give them to more dedicated gardeners—without feeling you have lost a major financial investment.

BULB DEFINITIONS

Most people, including me, use the term "bulb" to describe a plant which has underground food-storage capacity. Botanists, however, distinguish between the different kinds of food-storing mechanisms. True bulbs, such as daffodils and tulips, tend to be round and to have their food stored in meaty scales. Corms, such as crocuses, are generally flatter in shape and have their food stored in an enlarged basal plate.

Tubers are simply enlarged stem or root tissue and come in a variety of shapes. Though tubers are usually classified as perennials, many are marketed in bulb catalogues; those that require little care and are suitable for shade are described in this section of the book.

When you buy a bulb or a corm, you are, in a sense, getting a completely furnished house: the new plant is already contained within; it just needs to arise from its envelope of food storage. This situation can be used to great advantage by shade gardeners because no matter what the light condition under which a bulb is initially planted, it will flower for at least one season. Even if your garden is in deep, dark shade, for example, you can plant fall crocuses in late summer and enjoy their flowers a month or so later. Because there is no sun to allow the foliage to ripen, however, these bulbs will only flower once.

LIGHT NEEDS

Most gardeners, particularly those espousing an easy care philosophy, want to see their bulbs rebloom year after year. In order for this to happen, the foliage on the plants will have to capture some sun before dormancy sets in. This requires a bit of location scouting before setting the bulbs in your garden.

If your shade is that from deciduous trees, early spring bulbs are for you. These will complete their flowering and growth cycle before the surrounding trees and shrubs leaf out to form a sun barrier. If nearby buildings are blocking your garden's sun source, check to see if there is light bouncing off the surrounding walls. Often this will be enough to allow you to grow bulbs that will flower in subsequent years.

And even if a dense evergreen forest shades your garden, there may be a bulb or two for you. Late winter bulbs often bloom under such trees; the sun is so low at this time of year that its rays creep under fir branches. White snowdrops, yellow winter aconites, blue Siberian squills, and colorful crocuses are good candidates for such locations.

GROWING BASICS

No matter what the shade conditions, however, you will find that most bulbs require good drainage and prefer a medium-light soil. Generally speaking, bulbs should be planted at a depth equal to three times their height; in sandy soil, they should probably be planted deeper, and in clay soil slightly shallower.

The time of planting depends on the flowering period of the bulb. Again, in general, spring bloomers are initially planted in early fall, summer bloomers in the spring, and fall bloomers in late summer. Once established in your garden, bulbs can usually be transplanted at any time after their foliage has or is almost faded.

EASY CARE SHADE BULBS

The following bulbs are all terrific. There are some for winter, early spring, late spring, summer, and fall. Choose from each blooming category and you will have easy care color in your shade garden throughout the growing season. Unless noted otherwise, all are free from insect and disease problems. Sources are given at the end of the chapter.

ONIONS

Allium

Onions in the flower garden? It seems hard to believe when visions of vegetables or weeds in the grass come to mind. And yet, there are many species in the Allium genus that are exceptionally attractive and almost totally carefree flowering plants. With the right choice, you can have alliums in bloom from April to November. Though most thrive in full sun, the following will give great pleasure to shade gardeners.

Nodding Onion *(A. cernuum)* Native to rocky slopes and dry hillsides from New York

to South Carolina and west to British Columbia and California, the easy care charms of this extremely attractive flower are just beginning to be recognized. Shade gardeners will particularly appreciate the nodding onion's ability to flower with as little as two hours of direct sun. The plant is quite adaptable, growing on its own in exposed rocky beaches, cool mountain woods, and dry, open woods. In bud form, the flowers resemble large white drops; these then cascade open into a lacy spray.

Height: **12 inches to 24 inches**
Color: **White, pink, rose, lilac**
Bloom Period: **Summer**
Zones: **4–8**

Turkestan Onion *(A. karataviense)* A great plant for the front of the border, the Turkestan onion features plump, dark green foliage that forms ground-hugging arches. In the midst of these unusual shapes, eye-catching balls of flowers appear. These last for up to three weeks and then leave a handsome seed head before fading away. My plants do well in a bright shade setting receiving four hours of direct sun.

Height: **6 inches to 10 inches**
Color: **Pinkish white**
Bloom Period: **Spring**
Zones: **4–8**

Lily Leek *(A. moly)* Until I came across George Schenk's book on shade gardening, I had always read that this allium is a sun lover. Since Schenk insists it is fine for shade, I have dutifully transplanted some yellow lily leeks to add cheery color to the blue lungworts and pink fringed bleeding hearts in one of my brightly shaded garden borders. Mark McDonough, allium specialist and proprietor of The Onion Man, recommends lily leeks for dry shade areas.

Height: 12 inches to 18 inches
Color: Yellow
Bloom Period: Spring
Zones: 3–8

Lavender Globe Lily (*A. tanguticum* in the trade but actually *A. senescens*) I'm a sucker for phrases such as "flowers are long-lasting," "foliage stays attractive all season," and "rarely seen in American gardens." When I saw them all applied to the lavender globe lily in the McClure & Zimmerman catalogue several years ago, I immediately ordered the plant—to my great pleasure. This allium has dark green straplike leaves; round Christmas tree bulbs of flowers appear in mid- to late summer. The clumps increase in size each year, and mine have reached the point where they are large enough to produce a succession of blooms for six weeks. My plants grow in a bright shade setting with four hours of direct sun.

Here's what allium specialist Mark McDonough has to say about this superb summer bulb: "A sweet smelling nectar secreted at the base of each individual flower attracts ants, who take up temporary residence on the blooms until they fade. Spiders, too, seem partial to spinning their webs concealed within the flower heads. Like the pale purple blooms of Hostas, flowers of *A. senescens* show up best in filtered sun or in evening light. Perhaps this is why they are also visited by moths. *Allium senescens* is an entomologist's dream, as well as a delight for gardeners!"

Height: 18 inches to 30 inches
Color: Lilac, lilac pink
Bloom Period: Summer
Zones: 4–9

Thunberg Onion (*A. thunbergii*) The purple flowers on this late bloomer don't even begin to open until late October. Allium specialist Mark McDonough says that when he lived in

Seattle, he found that this plant would flower into December there. In his current home in Pepperell, Massachusetts, its blossoms last well into November. Plants, or information on where they can be obtained, are offered by The Onion Man (see address in Appendix).

Height: 8 inches to 12 inches
Color: Purple
Bloom Period: Fall
Zones: 3–8

Wild Leek (*A. tricoccum*) Native in cool, deciduous woods from New Brunswick to Minnesota and south to North Carolina and Iowa, this plant will bloom in heavy shade. Its leaves are considered an early spring taste treat. After these fade, flower stalks appear in late June or early July. Plants, or information on where they can be obtained, are offered by The Onion Man (see address in Appendix).

Height: 8 inches to 10 inches
Color: White, greenish white
Bloom Period: Summer
Zones: 3–8

Ramson, Rampion (*A. ursinum*) Streams of the small white ramson flowers cascade through English woodland glens filled with bluebells. Indeed, so aggressive is this member of the Allium genus that it is pushing aside the bluebell in many areas. This is one of the most shade-tolerant alliums; while I do not grow this plant, I think it would be perfect for tough woodland areas where few other spring plants thrive.

Height: 12 inches to 18 inches
Color: White
Bloom Period: Spring
Zones: 4–9
   (Pictured on page 92)

Lebanon Onion (*A. zebdanense*) An ideal

plant for a dry, woodland shade setting filled with humus-rich soil, this beautiful allium is covered with large, brilliantly white flowers in May and June. Within two weeks after the last bloom fades, the plant goes completely dormant.

Height: 12 inches to 16 inches
Color: White
Bloom Period: Spring
Zones: 4/5–8

(NOTE: To further explore the easy care beauty of the Allium genus, subscribe to *G.A.R.L.I.C.*, a quarterly newsletter for allium aficionados. For subscription information send a stamped, self-addressed envelope to Mark McDonough, 30 Mt. Lebanon Street, Pepperell, MA 01463.)

WINDFLOWER
Anemone

Covered with daisylike flowers for up to a month, these wonderful easy care bulbs look particularly handsome under canopies of trees or nestled in the green of early spring lawns. The foliage fades just as mowing season arrives.

Though I have never attempted to do so, others report that the bulbs can be potted and forced for winter bloom indoors.

Italian Windflower *(A. apennina)* A favorite at Winterthur, this bulb does particularly well when planted under deciduous trees.

Height: 6 inches to 9 inches
Color: Blue to white
Bloom Period: Early spring
Zones: 6–9

Grecian Windflower *(A. blanda)* More compact, earlier blooming, and hardier than the above, this is an early spring treat. I especially like the brightness of the white forms.

Height: 4 inches to 6 inches
Color: White, blue, or pink
Bloom Period: Early spring
Zones: 5–9

FANCY-LEAVED CALADIUM
C. × hortulanum

One of the few bulbs in this section that I do not personally grow, I include it because of its extraordinary good looks in shaded settings and because so many of my friends have success with it. Since it is widely available in garden centers, a low-maintenance approach dictates that you buy this tender bulb already potted and growing, keep it watered well during the summer, and then compost it after frost strikes. If you cannot find this plant locally, you can order it from several of the seed firms listed in the Appendix.

Mary Harper combines white Grecian windflowers with blue grape hyacinths in the shaded front lawn of her Princeton, New Jersey, home.

Height: 6 inches to 24 inches
Color: Flowers insignificant; foliage spotted
and streaked with combinations of
red, pink, silver, white, and green
Bloom Period: Summer to first frost
Zones: Nationwide annual
(Pictured on pages 19, 25, and 106)

WILD HYACINTH
Camassia

These northwest natives are usually
described as requiring full sun. In *Gardening
in the Shade*, Harriet K. Morse writes that they
are suitable in half shade or among deciduous
trees in high shade. That makes sense, since
the genus is naturalized in light woodlands.

Cusick Camass *(C. cusickii)* This northeastern
Oregon native appears to be the hardiest of the
species. When in flower, it is almost impossible
to tell the difference between this bulb and the
leichtlin camass. The two are among the few
plants that bear spikes of flowers in spring; both
are smashing additions to any flower bed.

Height: 3 feet to 4 feet
Color: Light blue
Bloom Period: Late spring
Zones: 4–8

Leichtlin Camass *(C. leichtlinii)* This bulb is endemic
to the Umpqua River Valley in Douglas County,
Oregon. One can only give thanks to the factors
that allowed such a lovely plant to develop and
flourish there. Note that it is not as hardy as the
cusick camass and that it comes in a greater range
of colors. The one other distinguishing factor, as
reported by Allan M. Armitage in *Herbaceous
Perennial Plants*, is that the withering flowers
twist around the seed capsule before fading away
(with that information I was able to distinguish
between the two in my garden).

Height: 3 feet to 4 feet
Color: Purple, light blue, white
Bloom Period: Late spring
Zones: 5–9

Common Camass *(C. quamash;* also listed
and sold as *C. esculenta.)* Native from southern Alberta and British Columbia to western
Montana, northern Idaho, and northern Oregon,
this unassuming bulb produces pretty blue flowers in late spring, and then its thin grasslike
foliage quietly fades away.

Height : 12 inches to 30 inches
Color: Light blue, white
Bloom Period: Late spring
Zones: 4–8

GLORY-OF-THE-SNOW
Chionodoxa

The members of this genus are among the
first to bloom in the garden year, bursting forth
with up to 10 starry blue flowers on each stem.
They thrive in any soil, requiring only moisture
and early spring sun. Somehow the individual
species have never acquired specific popular
names. The two species listed below are both
called glory-of-the-snow. They are easily
obtained and distinguished primarily by their
color. Try them both, either in your flower beds
or in pots on decks or porches.

C. luciliae

Height: 3 inches to 8 inches
Color: Light blue
Bloom Period: Late winter, early spring
Zones: 4–9
(Pictured on pages 41, 98)

C. sardensis

Height: 3 inches to 8 inches

Color: Brilliant blue
Bloom Period: Late winter, early spring
Zones: 4–9

At the base of a pin oak tree in her Princeton, New Jersey, garden, Mary Mills has created a beautiful spring planting of glory-of-the-snow and pink-tinged Lenten roses. For a look at this setting in October, see page 134.

SPRING BEAUTY
Claytonia virginica

This little flower is indeed a spring beauty, adding dainty charm in shaded woodland settings in southern and central Canada, all through the eastern half of the U.S., and as far south as Texas. It's also great massed in spring formal beds with its drifts of flowers filling in bare brown spots; come summer, the foliage has withered away and no sign of the plant is left. Another hard-to-find plant, this can be obtained through Montrose Nursery (see Appendix).

Height: 8 inches to 12 inches
Color: Palest pink
Bloom Period: Spring
Zones: 3–8

FALL CROCUS
Colchicum

Just as the garden party is fading, colchicums make their grand entrance on the scene. These fall-blooming corms produce large, elegant flowers in gorgeous pinks, whites, and lavenders. They are real show-stoppers.

Their foliage, however, is something else. It shoots up in spring and soon forms an unattractive mound of large, floppy green leaves. By summer, these have gruesomely withered away. Siting these bulbs in a flower bed is a bit tricky: you want to get the full benefit of the fall flower, and yet you also want to minimize the visual impact of the spring foliage. Each gardener has to work out his or her own compromise.

In addition to the two species listed below, plant breeders have developed several new hybrid forms. One of the most beautiful is called 'Waterlily'; this lasted only one year in my garden. Two much more reliable, and also quite lovely, hybrids are 'Lilac Wonder' and 'The Giant' (the last is pictured on the right).

Meadow Saffron (*C. autumnale*)
Height: 6 inches to 10 inches
Color: Light pink, white
Bloom Period: Fall
Zones: 4–9

Showy Autumn Crocus (*C. speciosum*)
Height: 8 inches to 12 inches
Color: Bright pink
Bloom Period: Fall
Zones: 4–9

CORYDALIS
C. bulbosa, C. cava, or *C. solida*

This is a simply enchanting spring bulb, producing feathery green foliage and a cluster of pink to purple flowers bobbing about as if they were a crowd of fairies at an annual convention. It is, however, not only little known but also unsettled as far as classification is concerned. The U.S. authority on such matters, *Hortus Third*, says that *C. bulbosa* and *C. solida* are the same plant; British horticulturists disagree and say they are two distinct species. To further muddy the picture, *Hortus Third* also notes that the name *C. bulbosa* has been used for *C. cava*. The truth is, you can't go wrong with any of these bulbs. As an added bonus, Princeton gardeners find they self-seed quite generously.

Height: 6 inches to 8 inches
Color: Pink, purple
Bloom Period: Early spring
Zones: Not fully established; certainly zones 6 and 7, and definitely worth a try in zones 5, 8, and 9.

Pink corydalis flowers bloom in the early-April garden of Louise Morse in Princeton, New Jersey.

CROCUS

Crocus

Crocus flowers yield only to tulips and daffodils in bulb popularity. In general, species crocuses have tiny flowers and are the first of this genus to appear, usually brightening up snowless landscapes in late winter. The larger-flower crocuses that follow and bloom from early to mid-spring are known as Dutch crocuses; these are generally hybrids developed from *C. vernus*. There are probably hundreds of varieties and hybrids available; all are easily grown and trouble-free.

Both kinds—species and hybrids—flower profusely in areas that receive winter or spring sun and then summer shade. Squirrels love these flowers; just make sure you plant enough for their dining enjoyment as well as for your viewing pleasure. Don't be surprised, however, to see crocuses blooming in spots where you never planted them, as they often reseed.

Easily grown in dry shade throughout much of the U.S., the lustrous violet-pink blossoms of The Giant fall crocus freshen up late-season gardens. The bulbs are pictured here with two long-blooming annuals: ageratum and sweet alyssum.

WINTER BULBS

(Bloom generally starts between December and mid-March in zone 6)

Crocus (*C. ancyrensis, C. chrysanthus* hybrids, *C. susianus, C. tomasinianus,* and *C. vernus* hybrids)
Atkins' Cyclamen (*C. coum*)
Winter Aconite (*Eranthis hyemalis*)

Snowdrops (*Galanthus nivalis*)
Bulb Iris (*I. reticulata*)
Siberian Squill (*Scilla siberica*)
Tubergen Squill (*Scilla tubergeniana*)

Care-free species crocus that are hardy in zones 4–8 and bloom from late winter to early spring include:

C. ancyrensis (3 inches to 6 inches, golden yellow);

C. chrysanthus hybrids (3 inches to 6 inches, white, yellows, blues —often veined in shades of brown to red-purple);

C. susianus; sometimes listed and sold as *C. angustifolius* (3 inches to 6 inches, bright orange-yellow); and

C. tomasinianus (3 inches to 6 inches, lavender). This last is usually described as the hardiest of the lot and best for deciduous woodland gardens. Squirrels supposedly do not like eating this flower.

In addition to spring crocuses, there are also several fall bloomers. As with the closely related colchicums, these bulbs produce foliage in the spring. The leaves are very diminutive, however, and do not blatantly intrude in a flower border. Since the flowers on these bulbs are also small, they are best placed in front of the border in an area that receives some spring sun. They are not as hardy as either of the above colchicums or spring crocuses.

Saffron Crocus (*C. sativus*)

Height: 3 inches to 6 inches
Color: Lilac, purple, blue
Bloom Period: Fall
Zones: 5–9

Showy Crocus (*C. speciosus*)

Height: 3 inches to 6 inches
Color: Lilac, purple, blue
Bloom Period: Fall
Zones: 5–9

WOOD HYACINTH

Endymion

Wood hyacinths rank among the easiest of all bulbs to grow. Once planted, they require no further care except for dividing overgrown clumps every five years or so.

Spanish Squill (*E. hispanicus;* also listed and sold as *Scilla campanulata* or *Scilla hispanica,* and sometimes described in literature as *Hyacinthoides hispanica.*) Wouldn't you know it: the easiest bulb has one of the most tangled botanical classifications! Able to bloom without any sun at all, the flowers are fragrant, look great outdoors, and are perfect for arrangements indoors.

Height: 8 inches to 15 inches
Color: Blue, pink, white
Bloom Period: Spring
Zones: 4–9

(Pictured on pages 84 and 142)

English Bluebell (*E. non-scriptus;* also listed and sold as *Scilla non-scripta,* and sometimes described in literature as *Hyacinthoides non-scripta.*) These radiant blue flowers carpet spring woodland floors across England and are just beginning to make their way into our country. They are more fragrant and also daintier than their Spanish cousins.

Height: 8 inches to 14 inches
Color: Blue
Bloom Period: Spring
Zones: 5–8
   (Pictured on page 92)

WINTER ACONITE
Eranthis hyemalis

In areas without permanent snow cover, the sunlight yellow of winter aconites popping up on bare earth or among dull brown grass is truly cheering in mid- to late February. The flowers don't mind being doused with late-season snow; as soon as it melts, they continue with their month-long blooming period. In one old neglected Princeton garden, these little bulbs abound in weed-filled beds. Nothing seems to stop them. After the bloom period, the handsome dark green foliage rosette slowly fades away.

Height: 2 inches to 6 inches
Color: Yellow
Bloom Period: Late winter, early spring
Zones: 4–7

SNOWDROP
Galanthus nivalis

While there are several good-looking members of the Galanthus genus, this is the only one that is profitable to propagate commercially rather than to harvest in the wild. Its nodding white flowers, tinged with a touch of dark green, always seem to conduct a race with the winter aconites to see which will bloom first. Both are very welcome in late winter gardens. There is

a pretty variety called 'Double Snowdrop' or 'Flore-pleno'; the species plant is so satisfactory that I have yet to try this newer version.

Height: 4 inches to 6 inches
Color: White with bright green markings
Bloom Period: Late winter, early spring
Zones: 3–9

DUTCH HYACINTH
Hyacinthus orientalis

The garden jury is undecided about Dutch hyacinths. Some people hate them for their plump, prim tidiness while others hail their fragrance, their bright colors, and their resistance to rodents. To help win more converts, breeders have developed a new strain called Multiflora hyacinths. These produce several stems, each loosely filled with flowers. While I'm not fond of these bulbs, I do think they add contrast and color sparks to brightly shaded beds of candytuft or pachysandra. They are also easily grown in patio pots.

Height: 8 inches to 12 inches
Color: A rainbow spectrum with only
         shades of green missing
Bloom Period: Spring
Zones: 3–7; annuals farther south

BULB IRIS
I. reticulata

Supposedly rodent-proof, these bulbs can also be forced indoors. I love their elegance and beauty and the fact that they are among the first flowers to appear. The flowers, miniature bearded irises, look particularly rich when nestled among a light fall of new white snow. Unlike most late winter bloomers, these bulbs do not naturalize; if you want more, you'll just have to plant more.

Height: 4 inches to 6 inches
Color: Purples, blues, whites
Bloom Period: Late winter, early spring
Zones: 4–9

SUMMER SNOWFLAKE
Leucojum aestivum

As the popular name implies, the flowers on this bulb resemble snowdrops; they are taller, bloom later, and do particularly well in warmer climates. There is a gorgeous large variety called 'Gravetye Giant'; I do not grow it but have admired it in other gardens.

Height: 12 inches to 18 inches
Color: White tinged with green markings
Bloom Period: Late spring
Zones: 4–10

LILY
Lilium

Beloved by deer and best suited to full sun, most lilies are not regarded as good candidates for shade gardens. My experience with the regal lily (see below) indicates that it is worthwhile to experiment with these bulbs to see if they are suitable for deerless shade settings.

Martagon Lily (*L. martagon*) A European native, this is the most shade-tolerant lily of all. Each stately stem bears 12 or more flowers. It is easy to grow as long as its roots are cool and damp.

Height: 3 feet to 6 feet
Color: White through black-purple
Bloom Period: Late spring into summer
Zones: 3–8

'Casa Blanca' Lily (Oriental hybrid lily) Descended from species native to the Orient, this hybrid was developed in New Zealand. Unlike most lilies, 'Casa Blanca' requires afternoon shade to perform best. Its large, richly fragrant white flowers open in midsummer.

Height: 4 feet to 5 feet
Color: White
Bloom Period: Summer
Zones: 4 (with winter mulch) and 5–9

Regal Lily (*L. regale*) This lily is regal in every sense. It was discovered in China in 1903 by legendary plant hunter E. H. Wilson, who risked his life to bring it out of the country. Hailed as one of the most magnificent and reliable of lilies, it is also one of the most fragrant. A summer without the luscious scent of this beautiful flower is a summer bereft of a special enchantment. Though most books properly recommended that this plant be grown in light or half shade, I placed my bulbs in a bed that receives three hours of morning sun and dense shade for the remainder of the day. The bulbs flower every year, though not as profusely as they would in sunnier situations.

Height: 4 feet to 6 feet
Color: White
Bloom Period: Summer
Zones: 3–8

Turk's Cap Lily (*L. superbum*) A native American, this lily flourishes in rich, moist, well-drained areas from southeastern New Hampshire to Florida, and west to Indiana. Its bright orange flowers tower regally over summer gardens. Rarely offered commercially, its seed can be obtained from Garden in the Woods and plants from The Primrose Path.

Height: 4 feet to 9 feet
Color: Orange, scarlet
Bloom Period: Summer
Zones: 4–9

GRAPE HYACINTH
Muscari

The bulbs listed here are all capped with cones of small, tightly clustered, bell-shaped flowers in early spring; in every case, the foliage has popped up the preceding fall. These pretty little plants are not only tough but also extremely inexpensive.

Armenian Grape Hyacinth *(M. armeniacum)*
According to *Wyman's Gardening Encyclopedia*, this is the most widely planted species. The bulbs increase rapidly.

Height: 4 inches to 9 inches
Color: Blue
Bloom Period: Early spring
Zones: 4–9

Azure Grape Hyacinth *(M. azureum;* also listed and sold as *Hyacinthella azurea.)*
George Schenk likes this long-lasting bulb and feels it is particularly suitable for shade gardens.

Height: 4 inches to 8 inches
Color: Bright blue
Bloom Period: Early spring
Zones: 4–8

Common Grape Hyacinth *(M. botryoides)*
The hardiest of the lot, this has been in cultivation for over 400 years. I have its bright blue flowers interplanted among the pale blues of the American Jacob's ladders. The rich green fernlike leaves of the latter completely cover up the fading foliage of the former. Recently, new cultivars have been developed with white or pink flowers.

Height: 5 inches to 12 inches
Color: Blue, white, pink
Bloom Period: Early spring
Zones: 2–8
(Pictured on page 96).

DAFFODIL
Narcissus

The terms "daffodil" and "spring" form a natural partnership across our country. Often books and catalogues describing these tough, elegant flowers feature swaths of bright blooms carpeting woods. And yet, daffodil foliage must have several weeks of good sunshine in order to develop bulbs for the next year's display. Since daffodils generally bloom from mid-spring on, many can find themselves shaded by emerging tree or shrub leaves before their reproductive cycle is completed. Thus, not all daffodils are for shade gardeners. In general, early-blooming daffodils and pink- and red-cupped varieties do best in semishaded situations.

In his book *Flowering Bulbs*, Theodore James, Jr., reports on two recent experiments on the long-term flowering performance of daffodils. Between 1972 and 1982, 200 varieties were left undisturbed at the Planting Fields Arboretum on Long Island, New York. The number of flowers produced by each variety was tabulated yearly. The Netherland Bulb Industry conducted a similar experiment over a four-year period at the North Carolina State University Arboretum. Daffodil varieties that appeared on both best-performing lists are as follows:

'February Gold' (8 inches, golden yellow);

'Flower Record' (16 inches, white petals with an orange-red cup);

'Ice Follies' (14 inches, white petals with yellow cup that whitens with age);

'Thalia' (16 inches, white); and

'Trevithian' (18 inches, lemon yellow).

To these proven stalwarts, I must add one favorite of mine—'Actaea', the *poeticus* narcissus. This richly fragrant daffodil has white flowers and an orange eye and grows 18 inches tall.

NOTE: All daffodils reviewed above can be grown in zones 4–9.

STRIPED SQUILL

Puschkinia scilloides; also listed and sold as
P. libanotica

This is a delightful, extremely inexpensive little bulb. It pops up in early spring, tightly packed with white flowers gently touched with a light blue stripe. By the end of May it has gone completely dormant.

Height: 4 inches to 10 inches
Color: White with light blue stripe
Bloom Period: Early spring
Zones: 4–9

SQUILL

Scilla

Both of the following are splendid, early-blooming bulbs—perfect for spots with winter sun and heavy summer shade. Plant them once and then forget about any further maintenance.

Siberian Squill *(S. siberica)* The electrifying blue flowers of this great plant are becoming increasingly popular in gardens across the country. While squirrels or other rodents may nibble the petals, the plant always puts forth at least some of its abundant flowers before being completely devoured. If left unscathed, the gorgeous blue blossoms can be picked for indoor arrangements.

Height: 3 inches to 6 inches
Color: Bright blue
Bloom Period: Late winter, early spring
Zones: 2–9

Tubergen Squill *(S. tubergeniana)* Not as well known as the Siberian squill, this bulb is particularly suitable for dark places or for long-distance viewing, as its white flowers stand out handsomely.

Height: 4 inches to 6 inches
Color: White with pale blue stripe
Bloom Period: Late winter, early spring
Zones: 2–9

TULIPS

Tulipa

Tulips are the most popular of all garden bulbs. They are nevertheless difficult for some shade gardeners. Deer love to eat them. Rodents such as squirrels, field mice, and voles enjoy not only the foliage above ground but also the bulbs underneath.

To other shade gardeners, tulips are a wonderful, easy care springtime treat. Since most

---

EARLY SPRING BULBS

(Bloom generally starts between mid-March and mid-April in zone 6)

Italian Windflower (*Anemone apennina*)
Grecian Windflower (*Anemone blanda*)
Glory-of-the-Snow (*Chionodoxa luciliae* and *Chionodoxa sardensis*)
Corydalis (*C. bulbosa*)
Armenian Grape Hyacinth (*Muscari armeniacum*)
Azure Grape Hyacinth (*Muscari azureum*)

Common Grape Hyacinth (*Muscari botryoides*)
Daffodils (*Narcissus* 'February Gold', 'Flower Record', 'Ice Follies', 'Thalia', and 'Trevithian')
Striped Squill (*Puschkinia scilloides*)
Kuenlun Tulip (*Tulipa tarda*)
Turkestan Tulip (*T. turkestanica*)

hybrid tulips are developed to flower for only one season, and come equipped with those flowers already stored in their bulbs, they can be planted in any shaded situation not ravaged by animals. When the blooms are finished, simply cut away the ugly, fading foliage.

If you would like to have tulips that do rebloom year after year, consider the following two, which grace my gardens. Both are species tulips (which means they are hardy and durable), and are quite inexpensive and bloom early enough in the garden year to allow their foliage to ripen before trees fully leaf out.

Kuenlun Tulip *(T. tarda;* also listed and sold as *T. dasystemon.)* The bright—and rather large for a species tulip—flowers on this plant rival those of early daffodils in spring cheerfulness and in attracting attention.

Height: 5 inches to 7 inches
Color: White with yellow center
Bloom Period: Early spring
Zones: 4–8

Turkestan Tulip *(T. turkestanica)* While this tulip is very multiflowered, its colors are rather subdued. Place it in a location where it can easily be seen so that you can appreciate its early bloom.

Height: 5 inches to 8 inches
Color: Creamy white with brownish yellow center
Bloom Period: Early spring
Zones: 5–8

ADDITIONAL SHADE BULBS TO CONSIDER

The following bulbs, corms, and tubers are not included in the recommended list for a number of reasons, the chief one being that I do not have sufficient experience with them. They are,

however, praised by others. Depending on your location or temperament, you might want to try some.

LILY OF THE NILE
Agapanthus

There is some confusion over the correct botanical names for plants in this genus. Technically speaking, *A. africanus* is shorter and *A. orientalis* has more flowers per stem. Several experts feel, however, that plants offered under either name are all hybrids. No matter what the classification, all bear lovely lilylike flowers on long, unadorned stems.

The dwarf (only 15 inches to 18 inches high) 'Peter Pan' is among the best of the hybrids. Its blue flowers will add color to the front of a shade border all summer long. Agapanthus plants, hybrid or species, are also excellent in containers (see picture on page 106).

In general, agapanthus bulbs are considered tender annuals and are sold as such at local garden centers or through bulb catalogues. There is, however, a new group of agapanthus (new to American trade, that is) called "Headbourne Hybrids." Hardy in zones 6–9, these were developed in Hampshire, England, in the late 1940s. British garden writer Robin Lane Fox believes they are actually selected seedlings, as he insists agapanthus species do not marry. In any case, these plants are sold by several of the mail order nurseries listed in the Appendix.

African Lily of the Nile *(A. africanus)*

Height: 12 inches to 18 inches
Color: Blue, white
Bloom Period: Summer
Zones: Nationwide, annual in regions with frost

Oriental Lily of the Nile *(A. orientalis)*

Height: 2 feet to 3 feet
Color: Blue, white

Bloom Period: **Summer**
Zones: Nationwide, annual in regions
    with frost

On a hot July day, the colorful foliage of caladiums complements warm red cineraria flowers and bright white agapanthus blossoms in a small, heavily shaded urban park in New York City.

SURPRISE LILY

Amaryllis belladonna

Similar to the magic lily (see farther down on this list), the surprise lily first produces green straplike foliage in the spring; this fades away by early summer. Just when all thought of the flower has disappeared, a large stem shoots up and is covered with beautiful lilylike flowers. This plant is best for warmer zones, while the magic lily thrives in more northerly gardens.

Height: 20 inches to 30 inches
Color: Rose red, pink, white, purple
Bloom Period: Late summer
Zones: 6–10
(Pictured on page 46)

ITALIAN ARUM

Arum italicum

Though this plant offers quite a lot—flowers, variegated foliage, and colorful berries—I'm just not taken with it. As an excuse for not having it in my garden, I can always cite that slugs devastate it, and I have far too many of these creatures around.

Height: 12 inches to 20 inches
Color: Flowers creamy white; foliage
    variegated white-and-green;
    berries orange-red in the fall
Bloom Period: Spring
Zones: 5–10

TUBEROUS BEGONIA

B. × tuberhybrida

There is no question that this is a beautiful flower. Given its handsome elegance, its maintenance needs—staking, regular watering, and feeding every three weeks—are really minimal. Its price, however, is not: over $25 per plant for the large-flowered varieties. If you want to treat yourself or give a really extra-nice gift, this would fit the bill. The plant is suitable in a border or a container.

Height: 18 inches to 30 inches
Color: Yellow, orange, red, pink, white,
    and gorgeous combinations, varia-
    tions, and mixtures of these colors
Bloom Period: Summer
Zones: Nationwide annual

PERSIAN VIOLET, CYCLAMEN

Cyclamen

Many gardeners are familiar with these flowers as house plants (*C. persicum*). The hardy versions feature dainty pink to white flowers that appear as small jewels in an autumn garden. Squirrels and other rodents leave them alone. As a further bonus, these plants have

SPRING BULBS

(Bloom generally starts between mid-April and mid-June in zone 6)

Turkestan Onion (*Allium karataviense*)
Lily Leek (*Allium moly*)
Ramson, Rampion (*Allium ursinum*)
Lebanon Onion (*Allium zebdanense*)
Italian Arum (*Arum italicum*)
Cusick Camass (*Camassia cusickii*)
Leichtlin Camass (*Camassia leichtlinii*)
Common Camass (*Camassia quamash*)
Spring Beauty (*Claytonia virginica*)
Spanish Squill (*Endymion hispanicus*)
English Bluebell (*Endymion nonscriptus*)

Dog-tooth Violet (*Erythronium dens-canis*)
Pagoda Trout Lily (*Erythronium* 'Pagoda')
Mahogany Fawn Lily (*Erythronium revolutum*)
Crown Imperial (*Fritillaria imperialis*)
Guinea Hen Flower (*Fritillaria meleagris*)
Dutch Hyacinth (*Hyacinthus orientalis*)
Summer Snowflake (*Leucojum aestivum*)
Daffodil (*Narcissus* 'Actaea')
Star of Bethlehem (*Ornithogalum nutans* and
   Ornithogalum umbellatum)

good-looking, glossy green, heart-shaped leaves. Montrose Nursery specializes in growing these plants from seed and offers the most comprehensive collection. For further information about the care of cyclamens, see "Growing Cyclamen" in the October/November 1991 issue of *Flower and Garden* magazine. The article was written by Nancy Goodwin, owner of Montrose Nursery.

Atkins' Cyclamen (*C. coum*) Popular in the southeast, this tiny gem is easily grown in well-drained, humusy soil.

Height: 3 inches to 4 inches
Color: Purplish magenta
Bloom Period: Winter
Zones: 4–8

Baby Cyclamen (*C. hederifolium;* also sold as *C. neapolitanum.*) Requiring dry summer shade, this flower is valued for both its lovely blossoms and its foliage, which is dotted with silver markings.

Height: 4 inches to 6 inches
Color: Pink, white

Bloom Period: Fall
Zones: 5–8

DOG-TOOTH VIOLET, TROUT LILY

Erythronium

These American natives are beginning to get more attention in the horticultural trade. As one of their popular names implies, they bear flowers that resemble flared lilies—but these are tiny versions that nod gracefully in spring breezes. Some writers say they are rodent-proof, others that mice love them. Slugs and weevils are also supposed to dine off their foliage and flowers. I grow the 'Pagoda' and think it a fine, care-free plant (probably because the slugs and weevils have yet to find it).

Dog-tooth Violet (*E. dens-canis*) George Schenk recommends this as being the strongest and hardiest of the lot. Unlike other erythroniums in the trade, this one is from Europe rather than the Americas.

Height: 6 inches to 12 inches
Color: White, pink, purple
Bloom Period: Spring

SUMMER BULBS

(Bloom generally starts between mid-June and Labor Day in zone 6)

African Lily of the Nile (*Agapanthus africanus*)
Agapanthus cultivars ('Headbourne Hybrids',
   'Peter Pan')
Oriental Lily of the Nile (*Agapanthus orientalis*)
Nodding Onion (*Allium cernuum*)
Lavender Globe Lily (*Allium tanguticum, A.
   senescens*)
Wild Leek (*Allium tricoccum*)

Surprise Lily (*Amaryllis belladonna*)
Tuberous begonia (B. × *tuberhybrida*)
Fancy-leaved Caladium (C. x. *hortulanum*)
Martagon Lily (*Lilium martagon*)
'Casa Blanca' Lily (Oriental hybrid lily)
Regal Lily (*Lilium regale*)
Turk's Cap Lily (*Lilium superbum*)
Magic Lily (*Lycoris squamigera*)

Zones: 3–8

Pagoda Trout Lily *(E. 'Pagoda')* This is the only trout lily I grow successfully. Its flowers are a quiet yellow and are lovely in a spring garden.

Height: 18 inches
Color: Yellow
Bloom Period: Spring
Zones: 4–8

Mahogany Fawn Lily *(E. revolutum)* This flower can be found blooming in spring forests from Vancouver Island to northern California. The cultivar or hybrid 'White Beauty' is highly recommended; it never made it in my garden.

Height: 7 inches to 12 inches
Color: White, pink, lavender, rose
Bloom Period: Spring
Zones: 3–8

FRITILLARIA

Fritillaria

The two popular members of this genus not only bear little physical resemblance to each other but also have different shade requirements. Though usually recommended for full sun, the crown imperial will do well in north-facing gardens or in high shade. The guinea hen flower, another sun lover, will do fine in dappled shade.

Crown Imperial *(F. imperialis)* I've never cared for this bulb, despite the brilliant colors of its flowers. To me, there's something unattractive about flower bells hanging beneath flaring, green foliage straps. Others think it a stately standout.

Height: 2 feet to 4 feet
Color: Red, orange, yellow
Bloom Period: Spring
Zones: 5–9

Guinea Hen Flower, Checkered Lily *(F. meleagris)* In England, the checkered, nodding blossoms of this flower are often naturalized among fields of daffodils. The subtle purples and whites of their upside-down tulip shapes blend well in such a situation but are, in my opinion, lost in a small shaded garden border.

Height: 12 inches
Color: Checkered purple, white
Bloom Period: Spring
Zones: 4–8

FALL BULBS

(Bloom generally starts after Labor Day in zone 6)

Thunberg Onion (*Allium thunbergii*)
Meadow Saffron (*Colchicum autumnale*)
Showy Autumn Crocus (*Colchicum speciosum*)

Saffron Crocus (*C. sativus*)
Showy Crocus (*C. speciosus*)
Baby Cyclamen (*C. hederifolium*)

MAGIC LILY, HARDY AMARYLLIS

Lycoris squamigera

My Aunt Olivet has this flower in her West Hartford, Connecticut, garden and it is always a treat to see its sweetly fragrant, fresh, lily-like flowers in a hot and tired August setting. It is also recommended as a container plant. As mentioned above, the magic lily is very similar to the surprise lily.

Height: 2 feet
Color: Rose lilac to purple
Bloom Period: Late summer
Zones: 4–9

STAR OF BETHLEHEM

Ornithogalum

Star of Bethlehem (*O. umbellatum*) was the only bulb on our property when we bought our long-neglected house, and I soon discovered why: it's an invasive weed, spreading every-where. One person's weed, of course, is another person's easy care perennial. Though the brilliant white star-shaped blossoms are attractive, the foliage looks like clumps of thick grass and gets some kind of ugly rust disease. This is not for me. I have read, however, of another species that seems worth trying. Though it has the same popular name, *O. nutans* is taller, has more flowers, and tolerates more shade.

O. nutans

Height: 14 inches
Color: White
Bloom Period: Spring
Zones: 5–9

O. umbellatum

Height: 6 inches to 18 inches
Color: White
Bloom Period: Spring
Zones: 4–10

SOURCES: Unless noted in a specific description, all of the above can be obtained from two or more of the following mail order nurseries: The Daffodil Mart, McClure & Zimmerman, Smith & Hawken, and White Flower Farm. Addresses are given in the Appendix.

FOR FURTHER INFORMATION about growing a wide variety of bulbs in both sun and shade, consult *Flowering Bulbs Indoors and Out* by Theodore James, Jr.

Prospect Garden, located on the Princeton University campus, has a changing series of formal beds. Annuals filling a shaded spot in late June include, from left to right, cherry pink balsam, light pink flowering tobacco, white wax begonia, and red impatiens.

It is a rare shade garden that does not have a flowering annual or two tucked in spots that once featured colorful spring-blooming bulbs or perennials. While impatiens and begonias are two of the most popular bedding plants, there are many other shade annuals that can add interest and variety to your garden.

Annuals are warm-weather plants that complete a life cycle in one entire season: germinating, flowering, producing seed, and then dying. In colder parts of our country, there is not enough frost-free time for these plants to encompass so much activity outdoors. In order to enjoy their full beauty it is necessary to start them indoors from seed or to buy seedlings from a local garden center in the spring. I always opt for the latter approach.

While buying plants is certainly the easiest way to get instant color (usually the plants are in bloom at garden centers), there are two major drawbacks: (1) it is much more expensive than starting them at home, and (2) the choice of annuals is generally very limited. If you want a cheaper, more varied selection of shade annuals, buy seed and follow the instructions on the packet.

While easy care shade annuals can be grown throughout the country, biennials are another matter. Several cannot survive bitter cold, particularly where there is no snow cover. Biennial seedlings that do overwinter generally bloom early in the garden year, produce more seed, and then die. The seeds, however, germinate, and before frost strikes, you will find many seedlings about your beds. These are best and most easily transplanted in late summer or early fall.

It makes little economic sense to buy biennials as plants, since they require two growing seasons to flower and since they are so easily grown from seed. Just buy a seed packet, open it in midsummer, and strew its contents about your flower beds. No digging, no fuss.

Remember, this is how nature instructs these plants to take care of themselves: tossing seeds about on open ground.

EASY CARE SHADE ANNUALS AND BIENNIALS

The following sample will ensure color in your shade beds throughout the growing season. I have grown all of them and recommend them enthusiastically. Sources appear at the end of the chapter.

AGERATUM
A. houstonianum

Found in flower borders across the country, ageratums have been bred in a range of sizes and colors. Usually associated with sun gardens—reflecting an ancestry in the blazing climates of Mexico and Central America—ageratums are excellent bright shade annuals. I plant them in summer borders after blue-flowering Jacob's ladders and Virginia bluebells have completed their spring show.

Ageratums' fuzzy flower heads turn a dirty gray brown as they go to seed; keep pinching these off and you will have a more attractive garden and a longer flowering period. Often, many of these seeds germinate the following summer (some in my lawn, of all places).

Spider mites like ageratums. These almost microscopic-sized insects suck juices from the leaves, dehydrating the plant and leaving telltale pinpricks on the foliage. If you keep watering your ageratum plants, you should find that they will weather such infestations.

Height: 5 inches to 30 inches
Color: Blue, purple, pink, white
Bloom Period: Spring through fall, if
               watered and deadheaded

Zones: Nationwide
(Pictured on page 99)

WAX BEGONIA

B. semperflorens–cultorum hybrids

This is another shade garden stalwart and, like the ageratum, has been bred in many sizes and color combinations. In my gardens, neither droughts nor downpours bother the wax begonia, and I have never seen evidence of insect chewing. Since it is not a large plant, you have to group quite a few to make a design splash in your garden. Tuberous begonias, on the other hand, are lustrously large; they are described in Chapter 7.

Height: 6 inches to 12 inches
Color: Flowers, white, pink, rose, red;
        foliage, green or brownish maroon
Bloom Period: Last frost to first frost
Zones: Nationwide
(Pictured on page 110)

CLEOME

C. hasslerana

Sometimes called spider plant, cleome is an old-fashioned native American flower. Thomas Jefferson grew it at Monticello, Virginia, and you can see handsome clumps of its pink and white flowers at the restored gardens there. Breeders have been busy with this plant, creating flowers in a greater range of pinks, reds, and purples than Jefferson ever knew.

Cleome blooms frantically until frost, growing ever taller as it does so. As the flowers fade, abundant seed is formed, often ensuring an ample supply of self-sown seedlings the following summer. In my garden, cleome blooms in areas receiving as little as three hours of sun. Seed production, however, is greater in sunnier spots.

Height: 3 feet to 5 feet

Color: White, pink, rose, purple
Bloom Period: Summer into fall
Zones: Nationwide

COLEUS

C. × hybridus

This popular plant is sold in garden centers across the country. Because you see the color of the foliage when you buy it, you can carefully place it to fit any garden color scheme.

As with all plants, coleus is genetically programmed to produce flowers and then seed. When this happens, the lushness of the foliage declines. Just keep pinching off the flower heads and give the plants a weekly watering and you will have beautiful foliage until frost.

If slugs are a problem in your garden, buy as big a plant as possible. These pests can chew a seedling to the ground in a matter of nights. Larger plants, however, prove to be too much for them to handle.

Velvety red coleus leaves combine handsomely with Palace Purple heuchera in the mid-September garden of Norman and Nancy Klath in Princeton, New Jersey.

Height: 1 foot to 3 feet
Color: Flowers, insignificant blue;
foliage, multicolor with whites,
greens, pinks, reds, scarlets,
browns, oranges
Bloom Period: Foliage will remain colorful until frost if flowers
are deadheaded
Zones: Nationwide

FOXGLOVE

Digitalis purpurea

Foxgloves are a wonderful example of how nature combines the beautiful with the practical. Their spectacular spires are the source of the heart medicine digitalis (a fact reflected in the botanical name of the plant). The darker the flower color, the more digitalis in the plant.

Native to Europe, foxgloves have adapted so well here that they are now naturalized in northern California, Oregon, and Washington—areas with cool, generally moist growing conditions. So accommodating are these plants, however, that they are grown in hot, dry Nebraska gardens as well as those in warm, humid Georgia. Just make sure the foxgloves have shade, are planted in good soil, and are watered.

Pests, especially spider mites, tend to attack once summer heat sets in. Fortunately the heat coincides with seed formation; I simply scatter seed about (ensuring many foxglove seedlings in the fall) and rip the parent plant out. Gardeners not bothered with such pests will find that trimming just the seed stalks will lead to repeat blooms.

Height: 2 feet to 5 feet
Color: White to dark pink
Bloom Period: Spring
Zones: 4–9
(Pictured on pages 9 and 19)

DAME'S ROCKET

Hesperis matronalis

This old-fashioned garden favorite should be in more modern flower beds. A European immigrant, it is now naturalized along woodland borders across the U.S. Just keep cutting the fragrant flowers, and the plant will keep producing more.

Height: 1 foot to 3 feet
Color: Purple, violet, white
Bloom Period: Spring well into summer
Zones: 3–9

BALSAM

Impatiens balsamina

Given a somewhat sandy soil and light shade, this plant will produce pretty flowers resembling miniature roses. Because they are tucked under the plant's top leaves, they are not attractive in arrangements.

Height: 1 foot to 3 feet
Color: White, pink, red
Bloom Period: Last frost to midsummer
Zones: Nationwide
(Pictured on page 110)

NEW GUINEA IMPATIENS

I. 'New Guinea'

These plants offer a big shade plus: colorful foliage as well as flowers. They were discovered over 30 years ago by Harold Winters and Joe Higgins while on a U.S. National Arboretum plant-hunting expedition in the South Pacific islands. Initially propagated solely through cuttings, New Guinea impatiens hybrids have recently been bred to produce enough seed for commercial sale. Unlike common impatiens, the New Guinea hybrids require at least four hours of daily sun.

Height: 12 inches to 18 inches
Color: Flowers, red, pink, ivory, blush, deep rose, bicolored; foliage, variegated lemon, ivory, pink markings
Bloom Period: Last frost to first frost
Zones: Nationwide

IMPATIENS, BUSY LIZZY
I. wallerana

Among the most popular garden plants, impatiens simply require ample moisture to produce a continuous display of colorful flowers. Spider mites and other insects may chew or suck the leaves; just keep on watering and the plant will rejuvenate itself.

Some people might eschew this plant because it is so common. Personally, I find it a great filler in shaded flower beds after the initial richness of spring bloomers has faded.

Height: 1 foot to 3 feet
Color: White, pink, red
Bloom Period: Last frost to first frost
Zones: Nationwide
(Pictured on page 110)

SWEET ALYSSUM
Lobularia maritima

This is a plant for small gardens; it would get lost in a grander setting. It is perfect for the front of a border, where it carpets all available space with a profusion of tiny flowers. Give it four to five hours of sun, or a very brightly shaded setting, and it will not only bloom freely throughout the growing year but also self-seed and return every year.

Height: 3 inches to 4 inches
Color: White, pink, purple
Bloom Period: Late spring to hard frost
Zones: Nationwide
(Pictured on page 99)

HONESTY, SILVER DOLLAR PLANT
Lunaria annua

The loveliness of honesty's seedpods—silvery white coins that glisten in a fall garden or in dried flower arrangements—often makes people forget the attractiveness of the plant's purple flowers in spring. Happiest in woodland settings with rich, loamy soil, honesty should be watered at least once a week if placed in drier garden beds. Since it is a biennial, some of the pods should be left so the plant can reseed itself.

Height: 2 feet to 3 feet
Color: Flowers, purple, white; seedpods, silvery white
Bloom Period: Flowers, spring; seedpods, summer
Zones: 4–8
(Pictured on page 19)

ROSE CAMPION
Lychnis coronaria

When the magenta flowers of this biennial cover the felty gray foliage, the result is gorgeous to some and jarring to others. Personally, I think it's great, though I'm willing to admit it is not subdued.

Another old-fashioned favorite, rose campion has been grown in European gardens as far back as the fourteenth century and in American gardens prior to the Revolution. Though mother plants can rot away in the heat and humidity of August, there are always enough fresh seedlings to grace a garden the following year.

Height: 18 inches to 36 inches
Color: Flowers, magenta, white; foliage, gray
Bloom Period: Heavy flowering for one month starting late spring or early summer, sporadic blooming thereafter
Zones: 3–9

FALL MALLOW, CHEESE MALLOW
Malva sylvestris 'Zebrina'

Often found in old European dooryards and herb gardens, this flower can now be bought at garden centers. Mine was labeled "Fall Mallow (Alcea zebrina)"; others have bought it as "Cheese Mallow." Variously described as a self-seeding annual, biennial, or short-lived perennial, it falls under the first category in Princeton. It has proven both pest-free and extremely long-blooming in my gardens, growing in a spot that receives three hours of morning sun and then heavy shade the remainder of the day.

Height: 3 feet to 4 feet
Color: White, pink, with petals veined in dark purple
Bloom Period: Summer through light frosts
Zones: 3–9

FORGET-ME-NOT
Myosotis sylvatica; sometimes listed and sold as *Myositis alpestris*

This biennial classifies as a "must" for spring gardens, especially wooded ones with lots of space. The forget-me-nots form mounds of feathery blue flowers that are impervious to pests and diseases. They are biennials, however, and in order to make sure they return to the garden yearly, it is necessary to give them enough open ground to seed themselves.

Height: 7 inches to 24 inches
Color: Blue, pink, white
Bloom Period: Spring
Zones: 3–8
   (Pictured on pages 59 and 86)

CUPFLOWER
Nierembergia hippomanica var. *violacea*

This Argentine native is a perennial up to zone 7 and an annual in colder parts of the country. Usually available in garden centers, it features mounds of fine, lacy green foliage dotted with light purple flowers. The cultivar 'Purple Robe' is particularly outstanding. Blooming tends to stop and the foliage to go limp in dry summer heat; just make sure to water frequently at such times.

Height: 6 inches to 12 inches
Color: Violet blue
Bloom Period: Summer, fall
Zones: 3–6 (annual); 7–10 (perennial)

CHINESE BASIL
Perilla frutescens

My husband hates this plant because it seeds itself throughout our lawn. The Eastern Native Plant Alliance has classified it as an invasive alien because it is choking out native plants located in the edges and clearings of woods. Obviously this is a plant that can take care of itself. And just as obviously, it is one that should not be grown in gardens bordering open woodlands.

In my fenced, in-town property, the purple foliage of this plant provides wonderful color in flower beds. The seedlings in the lawn, as I point out to my husband every year, die after repeated mowings. To reduce such rampant spread, just cut off the flower heads that appear in late summer. Otherwise, this plant requires absolutely no care. In heavy shade it will reach only about 1 foot in height and will produce very few seeds.

Height: 1 foot to 4 feet
Color: Flowers, pink; foliage, purple
Bloom Period: Flowers, late summer;
foliage, all season to frost
Zones: Nationwide

The purple foliage of Chinese basil is an excellent filler in a late August garden. It is pictured here with the purple-pink flowers of old garden phlox and the white form of big blue lobelia.

FEVERFEW

Tanacetum parthenium; often listed and sold as *Chrysanthemum parthenium, Matricaria parthenium,* or *Parthenium matricaria*

This is an all-time great plant, one whose virtues I have been proclaiming ever since Corinne Rowley gave me my first seedling from her West Hartford, Connecticut, garden 20 years ago. It is a plant that probably came over on the Mayflower, brought for its medicinal qualities (it is the source of a drug now believed effective in curing migraines). Depending on its location, it can be either an annual, a biennial, or a short-lived perennial.

In my garden, it is the last two. Feverfew plants that winter over start blooming in early June. The seedlings that make it through the cold months begin to flower in late July and continue to do so through several frosts.

The foliage is a rich green and the flowers are a beautiful white, looking like small daisies. Keep cutting them, and the plant will continue blooming. Though usually found in sunny gardens, this wonderful plant will also flower in shaded areas receiving as little as three hours of sun.

In the decades I have grown this plant, I have found only one insect to disfigure it—the four-

Cultivars of blue monkshood and white feverfew bloom gloriously in an early July trial garden at White Flower Farm in Litchfield, Connecticut.

lined plant bug. You can tell it's feasting on your feverfews when you see lots of little dried brown spots on the leaves. Fortunately, the bugs can be dispatched with one or two dustings of rotenone.

Height: 24 inches to 42 inches
Color: White
Bloom Period: Summer through several light frosts
Zones: 4–10

WISHBONE FLOWER

Torenia fournieri

This pretty little flower perks up both garden beds and containers as long as it is well watered. It often seeds itself, both throughout the summer and from year to year. As the plant ages, particularly with the advent of cooler weather, the foliage turns a lovely purple.

Height: 8 inches to 12 inches
Color: Bicolor flowers, primarily lavender splashed with dark blue and yellow; newer varieties white splashed with wine red or pink and yellow
Bloom Period: Summer into fall
Zones: Nationwide

PANSY

Viola × wittrockiana

Pansies have traditionally been an early spring delight, cool-weather plants that are able to withstand light frosts. Breeders have now extended the bloom period, producing plants that can flower well into the heat and humidity of July. Unless well watered, however, most pansies peter out by then.

Height: 6 inches to 8 inches
Color: Just about every color, including many bicolor combinations

Bloom Period: Spring and, if watered, summer
Zones: Nationwide
(Pictured on page 19)

ADDITIONAL SHADE ANNUALS AND BIENNIALS TO CONSIDER

The following were omitted from the recommended list primarily because I am not familiar with them. Depending on your location or temperament, you might want to try one or more.

PURPLE ANGELICA

A. gigas

Discovered by Barry R. Yinger several years ago in East Asia, the purple pompon flower head and foliage of this majestic plant are standouts in August borders. Princeton garden friends report that while its maintenance needs are minimal, it is difficult to grow from seed and that rabbits view tiny seedlings as a taste treat. These problems can be solved by buying large potted plants.

Height: 4 feet
Color: Purple flowers and foliage
Bloom Period: Late July and August
Zones: 5–8

FLOWERING KALE

Brassica × hybrida

Grown for its colorful, crinkled foliage, flowering kale is terrific as an autumn pot plant in dark, shady corners. Once severe frosts (and it takes quite a few) have knocked it out, just dispose of the plant and buy a new one the following year. If you try growing it from seed, you will find it attacked during summer months by cabbage worms and aphids.

Height: 8 inches to 20 inches
Color: Multicolored foliage in white, pink, purple, and green
Bloom Period: Fall
Zones: Nationwide in cool shade

BROWALLIA
B. americana

This plant is a stalwart in some gardens but just can't make it in mine. True, the first year I planted it in a back border, its lovely blue flowers were wonderful. In three subsequent years, the browallia was attacked either by disease or by spider mite and died within a month of transplanting. Easy care for some, but not for me.

Height: 10 inches to 24 inches
Color: Primarily a lovely blue; white or violet varieties also available
Bloom Period: Summer
Zones: Nationwide

TALL BELLFLOWER
Campanula americana

I came across the tall bellflower (it is recommended by the Abraham Lincoln Memorial Garden in Springfield, Illinois) while conducting research for this book. It is an American native with a wide natural range, being found in moist woods from New York to Florida and west to the Mississippi, and can be treated as either an annual or a biennial. Unfortunately I could not find a national commercial source for this plant.

Height: 5 feet to 6 feet
Color: Blue
Bloom Period: Summer
Zones: Nationwide

MADAGASCAR PERIWINKLE, VINCA ROSEA
Catharanthus roseus
Used in Asian medicines for centuries, this

plant was recently found to be the source of two major cancer-treatment drugs, vincristine and vinblastine. Gardeners appreciate its colorful phloxlike flowers, which have a long period of bloom (as long as the plant doesn't dry out) and an ability to withstand high temperatures and humid weather.

Height: 10 inches to 24 inches
Color: Rose red, pink, white
Bloom Period: All summer into fall
Zones: Nationwide
(Pictured on page 15)

FUCHSIA
F. × hybrida

There are supposedly 2,000 varieties of this lush tropical plant growing in gardens across our country. Most often, you will see them in hanging baskets so that you can better appreciate their gorgeous, drooping flowers. Somehow, despite all my watering, this plant just did not do well for me. *New York Times* columnist Linda Yang, on the other hand, rates it among her favorites.

Height: 2 feet to 5 feet
Color: Many bicolors with white, pink, red, and purple combinations
Bloom Period: Late frost to first frost
Zones: Nationwide

EDGING LOBELIA
L. erinus

This plant does particularly well in containers, and you can often see its beautiful blue flowers mixed with white alyssum and a variegated vinca vine. It tends to wilt in my shade borders, however, probably because I place it in rather thick clay soil that is not frequently watered.

Height: 4 inches to 5 inches
Color: Primarily sky blue, some cultivars in white, pink, or purple

Bloom Period: Summer to frost
Zones: Nationwide

FLOWERING TOBACCO
Nicotiana alata

The first summer we lived in our house, I grew flowering tobacco plants from seed by our front steps. In the early evening I would inhale the delicious fragrance emanating from these flowers. It still brings back fond memories.

The plants were leggy, however, and tended to flop. Aphids liked to chew on them. When we built an addition to our house, I moved self-sown seedlings to a back bed. When seen from a distance, I felt they looked messy, and I have never grown them since.

New cultivars have been developed, and these are supposed to be not only sturdier but also more colorful. The tradeoff is that there is no fragrance.

Height: 2 feet to 4 feet
Color: White or pink
Bloom Period: Summer, fall
Zones: Nationwide
   (Pictured on page 110)

SCORPIONWEED
Phacelia bipinnatifida

Found in moist, fertile woods from West Virginia to Illinois and south to Georgia, Alabama, and Arkansas, this native biennial is a staff favorite at the North Carolina Botanical Garden. It germinates in late summer and grows through the winter to provide a mat of lavender-blue flowers in mid-spring. Rarely offered in commercial trade, seeds for this plant can be obtained from Native Gardens (address in Appendix).

Height: 8 inches to 24 inches
Color: Lavender-blue
Bloom Period: Spring

Zones: 5–8

CINERARIA
Senecio × hybridus

This is a great container plant, often seen in city gardens, as well as a naturalized woodland plant in warmer areas of the country. It is especially recommended for San Francisco Bay Area gardens by Don Mahoney, nursery coordinator of the Strybing Arboretum.

Height: 1 foot to 3 feet
Color: Red, blue, purple, pink, white
Bloom Period: Spring into summer
Zones: Nationwide
   (Pictured on page 106)

NASTURTIUM
Tropaeolum majus

Best grown in bright shade, such as that found in northern exposures, nasturtiums provide cheery sunny colors. Alison Harris, my across-the-street neighbor, plants them in her front yard, and I love looking at them from my dining-room window. In my flower beds, however, nasturtiums have terrible luck, dying slowly from infestations of plant lice or ugly black aphids. Another plant that is easy care for some, but not for all.

Height: 1 foot to 4 feet
Color: Red, yellow, orange
Bloom Period: Summer to frost
Zones: Nationwide
   (Pictured on page 29 and 52)

SOURCES: Unless noted differently in the text, seed for all of the above flowers can be obtained from two or more of the following sources: Burpee, DeGiorgi Seeds, Harris Seeds, Park Seed Company, Pinetree, Stokes, and Thompson & Morgan. Addresses for these firms are in the Appendix

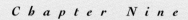

Chapter Nine

ASTILBES, FERNS, AND HOSTAS

Furry gray Dallas peers solemnly at an intense pink clump of Rhineland astilbe in one of the many lovely shade gardens Bonnie Stafford has created on her Princeton, New Jersey, property. The red plumes of Fanal astilbe and the dramatic foliage of Hosta sieboldiana *'Elegans' are in the background.*

The big three of shade gardening—astilbes, ferns, and hostas—are valued not only for their ability to grow in dark corners but also because they are fresh and attractive in summer, a hot time of year when most shade plants have either finished blooming or are waiting for the coolness of fall to look their best.

ASTILBES

Astilbes are beautiful Asiatic plants that feature good-looking deeply cut leaves and feathery plumes of lovely flowers. As a plant group, they are both incestuous and promiscuous—cross-breeding, hybridizing, self-seeding, and expanding with abandon. This has led to great confusion among horticulturists as to the correct identification of many plants and to almost anarchic conditions in the nursery trade as to what plant is being sold.

It is not unusual to buy two plants with the same name (as I have) and discover that they have different characteristics. In my case, the astilbes were called 'Deutschland.' Those from my first purchase have rather wimpy flowers but nice foliage; those from the second are taller, bear gorgeous plumes, and have nondescript foliage.

In truth, no matter what kind of astilbe you buy, you will find it will look good either as a foliage or a flowering plant. The fame and widespread appreciation of this shade gem is due to the work of Georg Arends (1862–1952), a German plantsman of heroic proportions. Arends spent his entire life tinkering with plants and creating beautiful new forms. Indeed, most astilbes sold today are classified as *Astilbe × arendsii*, in honor of the fact that they are the result of one of his crosses.

Astilbes have the general shade plant requirement of needing loamy soil rich in organic matter. They require a good deal of water, and if they do not get it, their leaves will first turn brown at the edges and then ultimately wither away. These are definitely not plants for dry shade!

Astilbes are also supposed to be fertilized regularly. I have never done this and am perfectly satisfied with the flowers my plants produce. Should you want to have a more spectacular display in your garden, sprinkle an all-purpose fertilizer about the plants in spring.

Finally, astilbes grow rather rapidly into thick clumps. To ensure peak flowering, these should be divided every three years. If you don't divide them, nothing drastic will happen—the flowering plumes will just get smaller.

EASY CARE ASTILBES

The following sample was constructed from three sources: my gardens, gardens pictured in this book, and recommendations by botanical institutions. All can be grown in Zones 4–8. Because astilbes are so variable, these descriptions are very general in nature.

'Deutschland' *(A. × arendsii)* As mentioned, plants sold under this name vary dramatically. All are easy care and have white flowers in late spring. (Pictured on page 125.)

'Fanal' *(A. × arendsii)* Arends first offered this plant in 1933, and it has remained popular to this day (it is recommended by the U.S. National Arboretum). It bears red flowers in early summer and has bronze-colored foliage throughout the growing season. (Pictured on the left.)

'Ostrich Plume' *(A. × arendsii)* When in bud, the flower heads on this astilbe arch gracefully. These open in summer to brilliant salmon pink flowers on stems that often reach 40 inches.

'Red Sentinel' *(A. × arendsii)* Another bright red astilbe, this plant generally blooms a week or so later than 'Fanal' and is about 2 inches shorter.

'Rhineland' *(A. × arendsii)* This plant sends up numerous spikes thickly crowned with beautiful pink flowers. Growing about 30 inches tall, it blooms in late spring or early summer. (Pictured on pages 120 and 125.)

'Pumila' *(A. chinensis)* Recommended by the U.S. National Arboretum, this is one of the most drought-tolerant astilbes. It is valued for both its shortness (only 12 inches high); its handsome foliage, which stands out in the front of the border even when the plant is not blooming; and its numerous raspberry pink flowers, which appear in midsummer. (Pictured on page 57.)

'Peach Blossom' *(A. × rosea; sometimes listed and sold as A. × arendsii 'Peach Blossom'.)* The first 'Peach Blossom' was introduced by Arends in 1903 at a meeting of the Royal Horticultural Society in London, and it made an instant splash by promptly winning a gold medal. It has ranked high in the hearts of gardeners ever since. The shadier the setting, the more the pink color in this astilbe. (Pictured on pages 9 and 18.)

'Superba' *(A. taquetii 'Superba')* Though often called the fall astilbe, bloom time for this plant varies from mid-July in Georgia to early September in Wisconsin. Its lilac pink flowers— crowning stems often reaching 4 feet—will last up to a week in arrangements.

FERNS

Definitely not flowers, ferns are nevertheless wonderful decorative accents in shade gardens. Their lovely foliage (fronds, actually) forms backdrops for all other flowers described in this book. This group of plants also offers one other bonus: according to Greg Edinger, museum educator at Bowman's Hill Wildflower Preserve, deer and other animals do not eat ferns.

Survivors of the dinosaur age, ferns are extremely tough and adaptable plants. To make them most at home in your garden, however, give them moist, loamy soil that is slightly acidic. The following sample was constructed from three sources: my gardens, gardens pictured in this book, and recommendations by botanical institutions. All can be grown in zones 4–8.

Maidenhair Fern *(Adiantum pedatum)* Praised as being among the most beautiful and elegant of the hardy ferns, this plant, 1 foot to 2 feet tall, is native to both North America and East Asia. Its foliage structure is quite different from that of other ferns: black stems appear to branch profusely and are covered with bright green leaves. This fern requires well-drained organic soil that should not be allowed to dry out.

Lady Fern *(Athyrium filix-femina)* Growing up to 3 feet tall and appearing as delicate, ethereal fans, these ferns are lovely in rocky settings or when contrasted with thicker-leaved plants. This fern is so hardy and adaptable that it can be found growing in the wild throughout the northern hemisphere.

Japanese Painted Fern *(Athyrium goeringianum 'Pictum')* The Japanese painted fern is both a beautiful and elegant plant, with a grayish green cast to its leaves and a maroon tinge on its ribs. Depending on its location, the plant will grow 1 foot to 2 feet tall. (Pictured on the right.)

Leather Wood Fern, Marginal Shield Fern *(Dryopteris marginalis)* Native throughout eastern North America, this care-free plant has shiny, often evergreen, 2-foot-tall fronds that some feel have a leathery appearance. Gardeners like it because it does not spread (the crown just gets thicker) and because its fronds are excellent in arrangements.

Ostrich Fern (*Matteuccia pensylvanica*) If you want a bit of drama in your garden, try this fern. Growing up to 6 feet, it is one of the tallest to be found in flower beds. Be warned, however, that it spreads quite quickly through underground runners.

In an early May garden, the pale gray foliage of Japanese painted fern almost seems to shimmer when paired with blue bugleweed.

Sensitive Fern (*Onoclea sensibilis*) Another invasive fern (but easily rooted out), this plant offers something of interest throughout the garden year. It has warm green foliage in spring and early summer and then, usually starting in August in my garden, sends up green stalks covered with spore "buds." These turn a rich brown and look elegant in flower arrangements as well as in bare winter beds.

Cinnamon Fern (*Osmunda cinnamomea*) This fern is a worldwide phenomenon, growing naturally throughout North and South America and East Asia. While its young croziers (or "shoots" as we nonbotanists say) are edible, they taste nothing like the spice designating the plant's popular name. The name refers to the brown, woollike fuzz of the fertile fronds, which looks like cinnamon sticks shooting up amidst the rich greenery of the 4-foot to 6-foot-tall plant.

Royal Fern (*Osmunda regalis spectabilis*) This is the native American version of the cinnamon fern. A beautiful, hardy plant, it can be found growing wild in shady, constantly moist sites from Newfoundland to Saskatchewan, and all the way south to Florida and Louisiana. In its natural woodland settings, it will reach 5 feet in height; in drier garden situations, it usually does not grow taller than 3 feet.

Christmas Fern (*Polystichum acrostichoides*) This native, eastern North America plant is one of my favorites and always shows up on lists of beautiful, easy care ferns. A friend pointed out to me that its stems appear to be covered with tiny Christmas stockings, hence the popular name. Boasting a dark, rich green foliage, this fern is evergreen and makes a wonderful addition to both winter and summer arrangements.

New York Fern (*Thelypteris noveboracensis*) A good choice for dry shade, and spreading quite rapidly in moist conditions, this eastern North American native has pale green feathery foliage. Rarely offered commercially, it can be obtained through The Primrose Path (address in Appendix).

HOSTAS

Hostas are simply wonderful plants. They are good-looking, tough, and adaptable, thriving in fully or partially shaded gardens from zones 3–9. Just give them good soil—rich organic matter that holds both air and moisture—and then forget about any further maintenance. (In dry spells, leaf edges may turn brown; this is not fatal.)

With the proper selection, you can have a hosta in bloom from late spring to early fall. And therein lies the problem. There are simply too many hostas to choose from. Not only that—there are also too many factors to take into account: leaf color, size, and shape as well as flower color and bloom time.

Even experts can't narrow down their favorites. To help gardeners make wise choices, The American Hosta Society in 1985 asked each executive board member to compile a good beginner's collection. The selections were constrained by price (no more than $150 could be spent for the entire selection) and availability in the trade. One of the more interesting findings was the diversity of choices, with not one hosta being named to all the lists.

The American Hosta Society also conducts an annual popularity poll among its members, with each being asked to submit his or her 10 favorite hostas. The names of the top 20 are published every year in the Society's journal. Once again, consistency of choice is not apparent. Hostas making the list one year will be gone the following year.

Paul Aden, a hosta enthusiast who has devoted over 45 years to breeding these plants, presented his hosta recommendations for the landscape in his authoritative work *The Hosta Book*. While many are popular elsewhere, several are looked down upon by other hosta devotees.

HOSTA LOVERS' HIGHLY RECOMMENDED HOSTAS

These are the hostas that appeared on the beginner list published by The American Hosta Society, on the Society's three most recent popularity polls, and among Paul Aden's recommendations.

H. 'Francee' features dark green, heart-shaped leaves with a neat, narrow white margin. Its lavender flowers appear in mid- to late summer.

H. 'Frances Williams' is named for an amateur gardener who started to experiment with hostas in her Winchester, Massachusetts, garden in the mid-1930s. Considered rare up to just a decade ago, it is now such a widely recognized beauty that it is a common offering among mail order catalogues. 'Frances Williams' has large, heavily textured blue green leaves marked with wide, irregular chartreuse yellow margins, and white flowers that appear in early summer.

H. 'Gold Standard' changes color during the growing season. Its medium-sized leaves start out a light green color with dark green margins and then turn to gold with a light green margin. This first appeared as a chance seedling in 1976 and has quickly become a shade garden stalwart. It has lavender flowers in summer. (Pictured on the right.)

H. 'Golden Tiara' has green, heart-shaped leaves with a gold edge. Its lavender flowers bloom in summer.

H. montana 'Aureo-marginata' has pale lavender flowers and large green leaves with wide, irregular yellow margins. It grows rapidly, forming a large mound. (Pictured on the right.)

H. 'Piedmont Gold' lives up to its name with yellow gold leaves that are creased and puckered. The flowers are white and appear in midsummer.

H. ventricosa 'Aureo-marginata' has large, heart-shaped green leaves with broad, jagged edges in gold to creamy white. Its violet flowers bloom in midsummer.

OTHER RECOMMENDED HOSTAS

The following either were voted number one in a hosta popularity poll or are recommended by individuals or institutions cited in this book.

H. fortunei 'Aureo-marginata' appeared on two of The American Hosta Society's popularity polls. The gold edging on its large, dark green leaves in spring turns cream as summer progresses. In September, the plant is covered with pale lavender flowers. This is the hosta Frederick and Mary Ann McGourty so beautifully paired with the lady's mantle in their garden in Norfolk, Connecticut (see picture on page 23).

H. 'Krossa Regal' has led the hosta popularity poll. With a vase-shaped form and silver blue, leathery, long pointed leaves, it's easy to see why it is a favorite. In late summer, lavender flowers appear on spikes up to 5 feet tall.

H. 'Royal Standard' is a popular hosta for both beginners and experts. It has medium-sized glossy green leaves and very fragrant white flowers that bloom for well over a month, starting in early August. This plant was on The American Hosta Society's beginner list and

Specimen clumps of hostas edge one border of Barton Rouse's Princeton, New Jersey, gardens. Pictured from left to right are Gold Standard, H. montana 'Aureo-marginata', and Royal Standard. The white and pink astilbe flowers behind the hostas are, respectively, Deutschland and Rhineland. Pink spires of foxgloves and brown fronds of the native royal fern rise in the background; multicolored pansies bloom in the foreground.

appeared on two popularity polls. It is pictured in the gardens of Liz Fillo (page 25) and Barton Rouse (above).

H. sieboldiana 'Elegans' has large bluish gray leaves and white flowers in early summer. This plant consistently appears on the popularity polls and was also on the beginner list, accompanied by such comments as "No collection complete without it" and "Best big blue at lowest cost." (Pictured on page 120)

H. 'Sum and Substance' has also been voted number one in the hosta popularity poll. It has large, heavily textured glossy chartreuse-to-gold leaves. Its lavender flowers bloom in summer.

H. tardiflora, a recommendation of both Paul Aden and the Boerner Botanical Gardens in Wisconsin, has a lustrous, dark green elongated leaf. As its botanical name indicates, it is a late bloomer, with lavender flowers appearing in September. Not widely available, it is offered by Holbrook Farm and Nursery.

H. venusta is a dwarf plant which was on The American Hosta Society's beginner list and appeared on one popularity poll. It has lilac mid-summer flowers and dark green foliage; at maturity, it forms a mound only 6 inches high.

THE AUTHOR'S HOSTAS

As a matter of personal preference I do not have any gold-colored foliage. Most of my hostas are monochromatic, old-fashioned ones, plants obtained from the flower beds of gardeners who like to share (or perhaps, who wish to make room for some of the newer, more dramatic hostas).

H. 'Blue Umbrellas' is a giant recommended by Aden and appearing on two popularity polls. It has large, blue-green leaves that are beautifully textured and heavily ribbed. Its white-edged lavender flowers appear in late summer.

H. lancifolia is a real old-fashioned species hosta that is considered too plain to be special. It has green lance-shaped leaves that form a large neat mound very quickly. In late August, it produces an abundance of long-blooming lilac blue flowers.

H. plantaginea is an all-time hosta great. It appeared on both The American Hosta Society's beginner list and on all three popularity polls used as sources for this book. As shown in the picture on page 79, it has large, shiny light green leaves. Its beautiful white flowers are both large and fragrant, and are responsible for this hosta's popular name: August Lily. If your *Hosta plantaginea* sets seed, as mine does, it is the species plant. If it does not, it is probably the cultivar 'Grandiflora', which is normally sterile. The former is often sold as the latter.

H. undulata, often called variegated hosta, is the most widely grown hosta, brightening up gardens across the country with green-and-white leaves and abundant lilac flowers in July. Perhaps its commonness is the reason why it is not singled out by any source. In my experience, this is the toughest, most easily grown hosta in town. (Pictured on page 155)

H. ventricosa is another tough old-timer. Henry Francis du Pont covered hills with this hosta at his Winterthur estate. The plant was chosen for its ease of care and for its lilac flowers in July, a time when few other shade flowers start to bloom. This plant made The American Hosta Society's beginner list and one popularity poll.

AND NOW FOR SOME SAD NEWS

Hosta lovers easily dismiss the words "slugs" and "chewing insects." Easy care gardeners cannot. The truth is that slugs, snails, black vine weevils, and earwigs devour hostas, either completely obliterating plants or turning them into ugly, emaciated eyesores.

Though yeast and beer are advised to trap slugs, these organic controls attract more critters than they kill. Poisonous slug baits are the next alternative. These have to be applied constantly—not a low-maintenance approach. Constant dusting with Sevin is recommended as a control for the weevils; the weevils will return again and again to the attack.

Thus I am forced to proclaim a hosta heresy: if your plants are devoured by pests, dig out the hostas and try different plants in their place.

While few if any plants can match the sumptuous foliage of the hostas, there are some good short-term substitutes. Consider three described in this book: *Heuchera americana* 'Dale's Strain', *Geranium macrorrhizum*, and bugloss (*Brunnera macrophylla*). In my gardens, these plants are not affected by slugs, black vine weevils, or earwigs. Deprived of the hosta as a food source, these insect pests will probably wander elsewhere in search of sustenance. After a year, plant a hosta in your bed again. For starters, try 'Sum and Substance'. This is supposed to be the most slug-resistant hosta in the trade. If it survives unscathed, slowly introduce others.

SOURCES: All core mail order nursery firms listed in the Appendix offer at least small selections of astilbes, ferns, and hostas. Crownsville Nursery offers the most complete collection of hostas (every one on the above list with the exception of the *Hosta tardiflora*) as well as a broad selection of astilbes and ferns. The Primrose Path offers a good selection of astilbes and a wide variety of ferns.

FOR FURTHER INFORMATION on hostas, see *The Hosta Book* by Paul Aden, and *Hosta: the Flowering Foliage Plant* by Diana Grenfell. For an interesting article on astilbes, see Allen Lacy's piece "The Ascent of Astilbes," in the January 1987 issue of *Horticulture* magazine.

HOSTAS GROUPED BY SIZE OF FOLIAGE

DWARF TO SMALL
These hostas are generally used as edging or small accent plants.
Their mature spread does not exceed 1 foot.

H. 'Golden Tiara'	H. venusta
H. tardiflora	

SMALL TO MEDIUM
The clumps on these plants range in size from 1 foot to 2 feet. They are perfect as dramatic front-of-the-border plants, as large accents in smaller gardens, or as mid-border plants.

H. fortunei 'Aureo-marginata'	H. lancifolia
H. 'Francee	H. 'Royal Standard'
H. 'Gold Standard'	H. undulata

LARGE AND SPECIMEN SIZE
These are all shade garden showpieces. Hosta clumps in this category start at 2 feet and can form mature mounds of up to 4 feet across. Flower scapes are up to 6 feet tall.

H. 'Blue Umbrellas'	H. plantaginea
H. 'Frances Williams'	H. sieboldiana 'Elegans'
H. 'Krossa Regal'	H. 'Sum and Substance'
H. montana 'Aureo-marginata'	H. ventricosa
H. 'Piedmont Gold'	H. ventricosa 'Aurea-marginata'

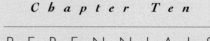

Chapter Ten

PERENNIALS

In spring, blue puffs of willow amsonia fill a shady corner beside Joyce Anderson's Hopewell, New Jersey, house. In fall, this shrublike perennial is covered with lovely yellow foliage.

Perennials are the antidote to garden dullness. They pop up, bloom, and then either disappear or display good-looking foliage while other flowers march onto the scene. In planting just a small selection you can have a changing procession of lovely flower color throughout the growing season. From day to day, week to week, your garden will present a different picture for you to enjoy.

What is astonishing is just how many perennials thrive in shaded situations. There are over 100 different plants mentioned in this chapter; due to space limitations, I had to eliminate many others. I like to think of the shade plants described here as being environmentally friendly; that is, give them the soil they require, be aware of their water needs, and then forget about any further maintenance, particularly with regard to the use of fertilizers or pesticides.

Several of these plants have built-in mechanisms that allow them to survive adverse conditions. The sieboldi primrose, for example, goes dormant in hot, dry spells or when spider mites attack; the roots hide underground and then new foliage emerges when conditions are more favorable. The majority of these flowers, however, are extremely tough plants that are simply not bothered by insects or diseases.

Many of the following perennials are probably familiar to those living near wooded areas. Gleaming white bloodroots, nodding Virginia bluebells, sprays of blue woodland phlox, and red-and-yellow American columbines are native plants which grow in spring forests across our country and which can just as easily decorate shaded garden beds around homes and townhouses.

Though most woods turn a monochromatic leafy green with the arrival of summer, the floral color parade need not stop in the shade garden. In addition to the wonderful hostas and astilbes mentioned in the previous chapter, there are over three dozen shade perennials described here that come into peak bloom in midsummer or after Labor Day.

Cultivation requirements for these plants are minimal. Most require good rich soil, the kind that drains well and contains lots of organic matter such as humus and peat moss. When planting, just cover the roots of each perennial with soil and then water. That's it. Any other special considerations, such as amount of shade and extra watering needs, are mentioned under individual flower descriptions.

EASY CARE SHADE PERENNIALS

The main problem you will have with these wonderful plants is limiting their numbers. Nursery sources and references for further reading are listed at the end of the chapter.

DOLL'S EYES

Actaea pachypoda; sometimes listed and sold as *A. alba*

With finely cut foliage resembling that of astilbes, and beautiful white berries with black "eyes," this is a handsome plant for deeply shaded situations. A native, doll's eyes thrives in woodlands from Nova Scotia to Georgia all the way west to Minnesota and Missouri. Give it a similar setting—rich organic soil cooled by overhead trees and mulched by accumulations of leaves—and it will be an attractive, easy care shade flower in your garden.

Height: 2 feet to 4 feet
Color: Flowers, white; berries, white with black dots in center
Bloom Period: Late spring
Zones: 3–8

LADY'S MANTLE

Alchemilla mollis, which is very similar to *A. vulgaris.* The two plants are often mislabeled and only horticulturists can tell the difference.

This should be a shade garden staple. Its tumbling, chartreuse green flowers are not only excellent in fresh and dry arrangements but also quietly complement other flowers in the border. Unless desperate, slugs and chewing insects stay away from it. It's no wonder that the Ohio Nursery Men's Association recently cited this shade lover as a plant deserving of more attention, one that is excellent in a front border, as a groundcover, or even as a specimen plant.

Height: 1 foot to 2 feet
Color: Chartreuse
Bloom Period: Late spring through early summer
Zones: 4–8
(Pictured on pages 18 and 23)

WILLOW AMSONIA

A. tabernaemontana

This is such a tough, easy care native that it now grows wild along roadsides from Massachusetts to Delaware, far from its native southern haunts stretching from Virginia to Missouri south to Georgia and Texas. It is perfect for a north-facing garden border, one with bright shade, in soil that is moist and well-drained. At maturity it looks like a small shrub and has a width equal to its height. In spring it is covered with puffs of light blue, star-shaped flowers, and in fall the foliage turns a lovely yellow.

Height: 2 feet to 4 feet
Color: Blue
Bloom Period: Spring
Zones: 3–9
(Pictured on page 128)

JAPANESE ANEMONE

Anemone

This is a genus that makes lay persons question the logic of botanical classification. There are many short spring-blooming members with daisylike flowers and tuberous roots that are usually classified as bulbs (see Chapter 7). Those reviewed here are tall, late-summer-blooming plants with lovely pink to white flowers resembling those on dogwoods. They are all easy care plants that will do well with as little as four hours of sun and heavy shade the remainder of the day, or bright shade throughout the day.

A. hupehensis. 'September Charm', one of the most highly recommended Japanese anemones, is thought to be a cultivar of this species. It produces silvery pink flowers for well over a month starting in late August. Give it a rich soil and water well at least once a week.

Height: 18 inches to 30 inches
Color: Shades of pink
Bloom Period: Late summer into fall
Zones: 6–10

A. × hybrida. Most other Japanese anemone cultivars are grouped under this heading. They come in many different colors and with flower forms ranging from single to semi-double or double. Taller ones will flop if not staked.

Height: 2 feet to 5 feet
Color: White, many shades of pink
Bloom Period: Fall
Zones: 4–9
(Pictured on pages 29 and 52)

Robustissima Anemone *(A. tomentosa* 'Robustissima'; usually listed and sold as *A. vitifolia* 'Robustissima'.) This plant is the toughest of the lot, sailing with ease through the heat and humidity of Georgia's summers and the cold and freezing of Minnesota's winters. After it settles into a garden, it starts to display take-over tendencies; you may find yourself weeding it out after you've had it for three years. I particularly like the seed heads, which open into white cottonball fluffs and look quite lovely in a bare winter garden.

Height: 3 feet to 4 feet
Color: Pink
Bloom Period: Late summer well into fall
Zones: 4–10

RUE ANEMONE
Anemonella thalictroides

This charming, diminutive spring woodland plant is native throughout eastern North America. Though perfect for heavily shaded woodland gardens, it also does well in heavily shaded formal borders. Its bright little flowers appear in spring. In particularly hot, humid summers, the foliage will go dormant.

Height: 4 inches to 8 inches
Color: White, pale pink
Bloom Period: Spring
Zones: 3–8

FALSE ANEMONE
Anemonopsis macrophylla

This Japanese native had found its way into American woodland gardens by the turn of the century and then somehow disappeared from public view. As its botanical name indicates, it is a miniature version of a Japanese anemone. Though it can take heavier shade, it also needs humusy, moisture-retaining soil. Unlike the Japanese anemone, the flowers on this plant face downward. With its astilbe-like foliage and late season bloom, the false anemone is a real gem for small shaded gardens and as a front-of-the-border plant.

Height: 2 feet to 3 feet
Color: Rose to pale violet
Bloom Period: Late summer into fall
Zones: 5–8

The first blossoms of false anemone rise above astilbe-like foliage on a Labor Day weekend at Garden in the Woods in Framingham, Massachusetts.

COLUMBINE
Aquilegia

There are at least 30 distinct species of this plant, many of them native to our country. My experience with columbines is limited to the three species described below. All are affected by an insect known as a leaf miner, a tiny pest that leaves telltale white tracks as it bores away through green foliage. Fortunately, the insect generally appears after the flowers have faded and seeds have formed. My easy solution is to cut the foliage to the ground and to throw away all infected leaves. Fresh new foliage usually appears. Even when it doesn't, the flowers have produced enough seeds to allow self-sown seedlings to bloom the following year.

The plants described below have different light needs. The American columbine is a staple in woodland gardens, in places that receive early spring sun and then shade from trees leafing out. The golden columbine needs a good four hours of sun and bright shade to lighten up a garden setting. The European columbine is the toughest of the lot; it actually seeded itself in the midst of an ivy patch underneath one of my fir trees, an area that only gets about two hours of direct sun and is heavily shaded the remainder of the day.

American Columbine (*A. canadensis*) Native from Nova Scotia to Florida and west to Minnesota and Tennessee, the beautiful red and yellow petals of this flower are a staple in spring shade gardens. "When established, it self-sows freely," according to Ken Moore, Assistant Director of the North Carolina Botanical Garden. He notes that it particularly favors garden paths, to the distress of some gardeners; "but," Moore adds, "what a wonderful wildflower to go rampant."

Height: 15 inches to 24 inches
Color: Red and yellow
Bloom Period: Spring
Zones: 3–9
   (Pictured on pages 11 and 59)

Golden Columbine (*A. chrysantha*) A southwesterner, this plant has proven to be adaptable in gardens across the country. In fact, it is so tough that it was chosen as a small group of American natives to be part of a recent spring display at New York City's Rockefeller Center. Its graceful flowers have long, slim, flaring spurs of palest yellow.

Height: 30 inches to 40 inches
Color: Pale yellow

Bloom Period: Spring into early summer
Zones: 3–10

European Columbine (*A. vulgaris*) This European flower differs from our native columbines in that its spurs are short and curve inward, forming in shape the top part of a hat while the flaring petals compose the brim (hence the British popular name of granny bonnets). The flowers come in a wide range of blues, purples, and pinks often combined with white. Given this great variability, the European columbine is not a plant for a formal garden. It is great in a more relaxed setting, however, as well as in cut flower arrangements.

Height: 1 foot to 2 feet
Color: White, pink, purple, blue
Bloom Period: Late spring into summer
Zones: 3–10

JACK-IN-THE-PULPIT
Arisaema triphyllum

This elegant woodland plant is native to over half our country, inhabiting areas from Nova Scotia and Minnesota south to Florida and Texas. The dried corms were once used medicinally by Indians. Today it is valued for its unusual yet elegant shape in a deeply shaded spring woodland setting and for its bright red berries in the fall. To some, these last are as spectacular as any fall flower.

Height: 12 inches to 30 inches
Color: Flower, light green; berries,
   bright red
Bloom Period: Spring
Zones: 4–9

GOATSBEARD
Aruncus

The two species discussed here are as different as can be. One is a tall, handsome plant that can form an impressive standout clump in a border. The other is a tiny creation with dainty foliage resembling that of an airy fern.

Dwarf Goatsbeard *(A. aethusifolius)* A newcomer to commercial trade, the small size and restrained nature of this plant make it perfect for the front of a brightly shaded border. As with its taller relatives, it bears plumes of flowers.

Height: 8 inches to 12 inches
Color: Creamy white
Bloom Period: Late spring
Zones: 3–8

Goatsbeard *(A. dioicus)* Into every gardener's life eventually comes the plant that dies a slow, ugly death despite the fact that everyone else raves about its beauty, toughness, and hardiness. Such a plant is the goatsbeard and its performance in my garden. Admittedly, it did produce plumes of white flowers in a shaded setting the first year; in each subsequent year, however, the foliage became horribly disfigured with a rust disease. I eventually threw the plant away. Still, the praise of this goatsbeard is so widely unanimous that I do not hesitate to recommend it to others. The cultivar 'Kneiffii' is smaller and has a more threadlike foliage; this is probably a good compromise between the species plant and the dwarf goatsbeard.

Height: 4 feet to 6 feet
Color: Creamy white
Bloom Period: Late spring
Zones: 3–8

ASTER

Asters are the floral glory of the fall garden. In the hands of English and German breeders

these native American flowers have been transformed into a wide range of plants varying in color and size. Just about all of these are sun lovers or tolerate only partial shade. I have grown the following three, however, in quite shady conditions. The white wood aster actually prefers dry shade, a boon in many drought-stricken areas. While the white sprays of the heath aster are spectacular in a sunny setting, they also enliven a spot that receives only three hours of direct sun in my garden. And the Harrington's Pink aster surprised me by blooming profusely with only three hours of direct sun in a brightly shaded situation (I had temporarily parked it in the area and had just never gotten around to moving it). Thus I can enthusiastically recommend the following three for shaded situations.

White Wood Aster *(A. divaricatus)* This woodland plant decorates autumn forests from northern New Hampshire to Ohio, south to northern Georgia and eastern Alabama. Yet another example of a native more honored abroad than at home, the white wood aster was used by noted garden designer Gertrude Jekyll in British estate gardens at the turn of the century while being relegated at most to wild gardens here in this country. With a profusion of white flowers in fall, it is finally beginning to be appreciated by American gardeners searching for easy care plants.

Height: 12 inches to 30 inches
Color: White
Bloom Period: Late summer into fall
Zones: 3–9
  (Pictured on page 35)

Heath Aster *(A. ericoides)* Native from Maine, Minnesota, and South Dakota south to Georgia and New Mexico, this truly widespread plant spouts sprays of branches loaded with tiny white flowers in late summer and early fall. I love it, though it is not the most formal of plants.

Height: 1 foot to 3 feet
Color: White
Bloom Period: Late summer into fall
Zones: 3–10

Harrington's Pink Aster (*A. novae-angliae* 'Harrington's Pink') Developed by Millard Harrington of Williamsburg, Iowa, this aster is covered with beautiful pink flowers for almost a month. The plant quickly forms thick clumps, which can be left alone or divided. When this aster outgrew its assigned space in my garden, I broke off two clumps (you need a sturdy spade to do this as the root structure is really woody). One clump was placed in heavy clay soil in front of a white brick wall, a spot that receives perhaps one hour of sun and heavy shade the rest of the day, and the other in humusy soil in a brightly shaded spot that receives about three hours of full sun. The first planting was anemic at best and the second thrived so well that I was soon dividing it again—but this time to give clumps to friends.

Height: 3 feet to 5 feet
Color: Pink
Bloom Period: Late summer into fall
Zones: 4–9

In early October, pink flowers of hardy begonia circle the base of a pin oak tree in the Princeton, New Jersey, garden of Mary Mills. For a look at this setting in late March, see page 98.

HARDY BEGONIA
B. grandis

Many who grow angel wing begonias indoors may be surprised to learn that there is a very similar plant that is hardy outdoors. First brought to public attention in 1804 by Kew Gardens in England, the plant was rarely grown by the beginning of this century. Why this is so is a mystery. The plant features not only good looks—beautiful pink flowers and handsome leaves with brilliant red undersides—but also a fall bloom period, a time when few plants start to flower. The only possible complaint about this plant is that it seeds itself readily; the seedlings, however, are easily yanked out. As an experiment, I placed this plant in two different heavy shade situations: one area had thick clay soil and the other rich, humusy soil. While the hardy begonia will grow in the former setting, it produces very few flowers; it thrives in the latter.

Height: 18 inches to 24 inches
Color: Pink, white
Bloom Period: Late summer into fall
Zones: 5–8

BUGLOSS
Brunnera macrophylla

Large, deep green heart-shaped leaves make this a wonderful foliage plant. In spring, it bears masses of warm blue flowers that look like for-get-me-nots. Though it does best in humusy soil that is well watered, I have successfully grown it in rather heavy clay soil with little watering. In this last situation, however, the leaves tend to revolt in the heat of August and turn rather ugly with splotches of black throughout. Slugs will nibble at this plant but they do not eat it to the ground as they do with so many hostas.

Height: 12 inches to 18 inches
Color: Blue
Bloom Period: Spring
Zones: 3–9
  (Pictured on page 155)

CUCKOO FLOWER
Cardamine pratensis

Now here's a garden mystery. This plant grows throughout the Northern Hemisphere, in Europe, Asia, and the Americas. That kind of geographical distribution guarantees that the plant is easy care. It also happens to be exceptionally good-looking, particularly 'Flore Pleno', the double form that I grow. Here's what L. H. Bailey had to say about it in the early part of this century: "It is an excellent little plant to grow in moist places … [and] … is also useful in drier places." And yet, somehow this wonderful spring charmer with diminutive evergreen foliage has almost disappeared from the garden scene. I have been able to track down only one source: Andrew E. Smith's Berkshire Flower Farm (see address in Appendix). In addition, Garden in the Woods is considering propagating the plant. I'm sure that once the word spreads about the cuckoo flower's good looks and ease of care, it will once again claim pride of place in American gardens.

Height: 8 inches to 12 inches
Color: Pink

Popular in European gardens but rarely found in American ones, the delicate pink blossoms of the deer-resistant cuckoo flower flourish in a May border in Princeton, New Jersey.

Bloom Period: Spring
Zones: 3–9

TURTLEHEAD
Chelone

These native American plants like moist, humusy soil and will do well in such a situation even with slugs lurking about. Both plants described here flower in my garden in a brightly shaded spot that receives less than two hours of direct sun.

White Turtlehead (*C. glabra*) Native from Newfoundland to Georgia, west to Minnesota and Missouri, this turtlehead has rather skimpy foliage. I have placed it in the rear of the border so that its lovely white flowers can peep over the plants in front of it.

Height: 24 inches to 36 inches
Color: Creamy white
Bloom Period: Late summer
Zones: 4–8

Pink Turtlehead *(C. lyonii)* Found in the mountains of the Carolinas and Tennessee, this plant has dark glossy green foliage which pairs well with that of hostas. Though the flowers are not as large as those on the white turtlehead, they more than compensate by blooming for a week or two longer.

Height: 16 inches to 36 inches
Color: Pink, rosy purple
Bloom Period: Late summer
Zones: 4–9

BUGBANE

Cimicifuga

These tall plants send up waving wands of white flowers that add grace and elegance to shade gardens. Though the two described below prefer similar situations—moist, humusy soil in shaded areas—they hail from very different parts of the world.

Black Cohosh *(C. racemosa)* A native American, this plant grows wild from Massachusetts to Ontario, south to Georgia, Tennessee, and Missouri. Its white spires of flowers are a staple of the summer shade garden.

Height: 5 feet to 7 feet
Color: White
Bloom Period: Summer
Zones: 3–9

Bugbane *(C. simplex* 'The Pearl')* This plant hails from northwestern Asia, in areas from

White spires of the inappropriately nicknamed black cohosh soar above a pink froth of coral bells and bright red splashes of bee balm in the late June garden of David and John Jacobus in Princeton, New Jersey.

Siberia to Japan. It is one of the last plants to bloom in the garden; for this reason, it may be unsuitable for gardens in zones 3 and 4 as the flowers could be smothered by snow. Its long (1 foot in my garden; supposedly up to 2 feet in others) slim pokes of feathery white flowers are eye-catching in mid-October. They are also quite handsome in arrangements. Even before the flowers burst open, however, the greenish white buds are attractive.

Height: 2 feet to 4 feet
Color: White
Bloom Period: Fall
Zones: 3–8

LILY-OF-THE-VALLEY
Convallaria majalis

This old-fashioned plant was a favorite of Henry Francis du Pont. It has thrived on his estate at Winterthur since before he was born. He loved walking among its fragrant white flowers as he and his father strolled about the spring woods. Later, when he was at Groton boarding school, his mother would send him sprigs to ease his homesickness.

Height: 8 inches to 12 inches
Color: White
Bloom Period: Spring
Zones: 3–8

CORYDALIS
Corydalis

Closely related to the fringed bleeding hearts and Dutchman's breeches, the flowers in this genus are colorful, good-looking, and exceptionally easy care. Shade gardeners are just beginning to appreciate the many fine attributes of the genus, and nurseries are finally offering the plants commercially. I have yet to find a pest that bothers either of the following plants, both of which can grow in heavily shaded as well as brightly shaded situations. For best results, make sure the soil is rich and humusy.

Fernleaf Corydalis (*C. cheilanthifolia*) It appears that Henry Francis du Pont was the first American gardener to grow this wonderful Chinese native. While its spikes of bright yellow flowers are attractive in spring, its chief claim to garden fame is its delicate, feathery foliage. The fernleaf corydalis has grown unattended for over 50 years at du Pont's Winterthur estate: how easy care can a plant get?

Height: 12 inches
Color: Yellow
Bloom Period: Spring
Zones: 5–10

Yellow Corydalis (*C. lutea*) This should be a staple in every shade garden. In my borders, it blooms steadily from late May into September. Depending on heat and rainfall, it will sometimes go on flowering into October. Should you visit England, you will see this plant growing in sunny sidewalk cracks. That's how tough it is. In my garden, it flowers without any direct sun—that's how adaptable it is. All this and good-looking foliage too.

Height: 9 inches to 15 inches
Color: Yellow
Bloom Period: Late spring through much, if not all, of summer
Zones: 5–9
(Pictured on page 14)

BLEEDING HEART
Dicentra

The *Dicentra* genus blesses gardens with beautiful, sturdy plants that can tolerate heavy shade when given rich, consistently moist soil. There are distinct differences between the eastern (Asian) and western (American) members. After a spectacular spring show, the Chinese bleeding heart goes dormant. Most American members of the genus, on the other hand, have less showy flowers but will often bloom sporadically through summer and have lovely blue-green foliage that adds good looks to flower borders and arrangements.

Dutchman's Breeches (*D. cucullaria*) This plant shares the dormancy trait of the Chinese bleeding heart and the dainty flowers and fernlike foliage of the other American natives. It appears to be more suited to midwestern gardens than the fringed bleeding heart.

Height: 8 inches to 12 inches
Color: White
Bloom Period: Spring
Zones: 3–8
   (Pictured on page 45)

Fringed Bleeding Heart *(D. eximia)* Growing wild from New York to Georgia, this is a great, easy care American native plant. To me, the flowers resemble tiny pink teardrops rather than bleeding hearts. Breeders have developed many cultivars that feature more profuse blossoms in white or in richer shades of pink. Whether you opt for a cultivar or a species plant, you will have a terrific shade garden flower.

Height: 9 inches to 18 inches
Color: Pink, white
Bloom Period: Late spring to fall
Zones: 3–9
   (Pictured on pages 9 and 14)

Western Bleeding Heart *(D. formosa)* Native from British Columbia to central California, this bleeding heart cannot take the humidity of the East Coast. Otherwise it is indistinguishable—except to an expert—from the fringed bleeding heart. Indeed, many cultivars are actually hybrids between the two species.

Height: 12 inches to 18 inches
Color: Pink
Bloom Period: Spring
Zones: 3–10

Chinese Bleeding Heart *(D. spectabilis)* Plant hunter Robert Fortune discovered this plant in Japan and brought it to England, where it first flowered in 1847. Its large pink-and-white flowers, appearing as delicate valentine hearts drooping from large, light green foliage, became an instant favorite both there and, soon afterwards, in the U.S. Writing at the begin-

ning of this century, L. H. Bailey called it "one of the choicest memories of old-fashioned gardens." It remains so to this day.

Height: 18 inches to 30 inches
Color: Deep pink with white markings
Bloom Period: Spring
Zones: 3–9

EPIMEDIUM, BARRENWORT
Epimedium

Epimediums are short, front-of-the-border plants with colorful spring flowers and good-looking heart-shaped leaves. At the beginning of this century, L. H. Bailey's *Standard Cyclopedia of Horticulture* was declaring that epimediums were among the "daintiest and most interesting plants that can be grown in the hardy border." Today's shade gardeners add to such praise the facts that epimediums grow in just about any soil and, perhaps even more important, thrive in dry conditions.

Supposedly, epimediums are disease- and pest-free. This has not been the case in my garden. One clump, planted underneath a fir tree, is steadily and persistently chewed by what appear to be black vine beetles. By the end of the garden season the foliage looks pretty battered. If I felt like it, I could simply cut the leaves away and have a neater-looking clump. I have also had rust on the foliage of the bishop's cap epimedium. In this latter case, the leaves look so ugly and ravaged that I have cut them to the ground—with no apparent detriment to the plant the following year. It seems to me that the rust problems are particularly acute in wet, humid summers.

I cite the above two examples not to discourage gardeners from growing epimediums but simply to let them know that if such problems occur it is the fault of the environment, not the gardener. Most of my epimediums—and I have many planted about my property—are not only trouble-free but also beautiful shade plants. It's hard to imagine a shade garden without them.

Longspur Epimedium *(E. grandiflorum)* Recommended by the U.S. National Arboretum, this is one of the largest in the genus. It is also noted for its flaring spurs, much like those on American columbines.

Height: 12 inches to 18 inches
Color: Rose red, white, and pale yellow
Bloom Period: Spring
Zones: 4–8

Algerian Epimedium *(E. perralderianum)* This is a breakaway epimedium, the only member of the genus found growing on the African continent. It is also a plant that carpets Muir Woods outside of San Francisco and that thrives in the Princeton, New Jersey, garden of Mary Mills. Obviously, it does well in a variety of climates. Unfortunately, this epimedium is not widely available. It is one of the parents, however, of the more popular hybrid cultivar 'Frohnleiten.'

Height: 10 inches to 12 inches
Color: Yellow
Bloom Period: Spring
Zones: 5–9

Persian Epimedium *(E. pinnatum)* This is among the shortest of the epimediums and has lovely yellow flowers.

Height: 8 inches to 12 inches
Color: Yellow
Bloom Period: Spring
Zones: 4–9

Bishop's Cap *(E. × rubrum)* Probably the most widely offered epimedium, bishop's cap bears lovely multicolored flowers in spring. Its

foliage, tinged with red, turns a reddish brown in fall.

Height: 6 inches to 12 inches
Color: Yellow and pink
Bloom Period: Spring
Zones: 4–8
   (Pictured on page 14)

Yellow Epimedium *(E. × versicolor* 'Sulphureum') This is supposed to be the toughest of the lot, the epimedium that best tolerates dry shady conditions and the poorest soil.

Height: 12 inches to 18 inches
Color: Yellow
Bloom Period: Spring
Zones: 4–8

White Epimedium *(E. × youngianum* 'Niveum') Prized for its daintiness and its lovely starry white flowers, this plant blooms later than the other epimediums.

Height: 6 inches to 8 inches
Color: White
Bloom Period: Spring
Zones: 4–8

BONESET, EUPATORIUM

Eupatorium

Bonesets grow wild across the U.S., with most blooming in late summer and early fall. They bear a profusion of fluffy flowers in whites, blues, mauves, and purples. Until recently, they were dismissed as wildflowers and not suitable for borders. Under the impetus of the New American Garden look, featuring low-maintenance plants and developed by landscape architects James A. van Sweden and Wolfgang Oehme, the easy care nature and stately attractiveness of the *Eupatorium* genus has begun to attract much attention. Though most eupatoriums are for partially shaded gardens (about four to five hours of sun), the white snakeroot will flower in heavy shade with only two hours of sun.

Hardy Ageratum (*E. coelestinum*)

This, in my experience, is the most invasive plant of the genus. It spreads by underground runners, particularly when grown in rich humusy soil. I have it planted in an area packed with thick clay, and it still manages to get around quite a bit. Come mid-August, I know why I tolerate its invasiveness: it begins a six-week bloom of light blue flowers that are wonderful in the garden and great in arrangements.

Over the years, I have noticed attacks by the four-lined plant bug. If it is serious—that is, when the foliage becomes covered with little brown dots and eventually withers—I dust the plants once or twice with rotenone and that solves the problem.

Height: 1 foot to 3 feet
Color: Blue
Bloom Period: Late summer into fall
Zones: 6–10

Hollow Joe-Pye Weed (*E. fistulosum*)

This is a garden giant, a tall, stately plant crowned with a large arc of dusty rose flowers about which bees constantly hum and flutter. According to The Primrose Path catalogue, this plant can be cut back almost to ground level in June to produce shorter, bushier plants. I have cut off its magnificent central flower head in August and have noted that side shoots bear blossoms well into September.

Height: 6 feet to 10 feet
Color: Dusty rose

Bloom Period: Summer into fall
Zones: 3–10

Joe-Pye Weed (*E. purpureum*)

According to Allan Armitage, this plant is an architectural building block of British gardens. It is one of Linda Yang's favorite shade plants in her small Manhattan garden. Very similar to the hollow Joe-Pye weed, it differs only in being a little bit shorter and having a richer purple color in its flowers.

Height: 4 feet to 7 feet
Color: Purple
Bloom Period: Late summer into fall
Zones: 4–9

White Snakeroot (*E. rugosum*)

This is another invasive member of the genus. Give it

Hollow Joe-Pye weed 'Gateway' and hardy ageratum create a spectacular display in late August at the U.S. National Arboretum in Washington, D.C.

PERENNIAL GIANTS

For a dramatic background setting or for striking accent plants, consider the following perennials for your shade borders. All grow 6 feet or taller.

LATE SPRING:
Goatsbeard (*Aruncus dioicus*)

SUMMER:
Black Cohosh (*Cimicifuga racemosa*)

LATE SUMMER:
Hollow Joe-Pye Weed
(*Eupatorium fistulosum*)

FALL:
Green Coneflower (*Rudbeckia laciniata*)

dense, dry shade, however, and it will not spread unduly while brightening up the late-season garden with lots of fluffy white flowers.

Height: 30 inches to 50 inches
Color: White
Bloom Period: Late summer into fall
Zones: 3–9

FALSE BABY'S BREATH
Galium mollugo 'Victor Jones'

This close cousin of sweet woodruff is a superb, easy care plant for both partial and fairly heavy shade. A selection chosen by the late Victor Jones of Mentor, Ohio, it is currently an exclusive offering of the nearby mail order firm, Bluestone Perennials. A profusion of tiny starry white flowers bloom throughout summer and into frost. These look especially charming when cushioned by the large, dark green leaves of bugloss.

Height: 3 feet
Color: White
Bloom Period: All summer into fall
Zones: 3–8

HARDY GERANIUM
Geranium

Long grown in British gardens and ideally suited for American gardens, hardy geraniums are perennial plants that differ quite markedly from the popular summer annual geranium (botanically speaking, the last is a *Pelargonium*). The hardy geraniums bear small flowers in whites, pinks, purples, and blues and are known for their good-looking foliage, whereas the annual plants are characterized by large red and orange flowers and rather gawky foliage. While there are over 200 species of the hardy geraniums, I can only vouch for the following. All are excellent garden plants—beautiful, trouble-free, and long blooming.

Bigroot Geranium (*G. macrorrhizum*) One of the easiest geraniums to grow, this plant also produces one of the best foliage displays—large, nicely rounded mounds of 6-inch-to-8-inch-wide leaves. In spring, these are covered with small flowers. Given its ease of care and good looks, breeders have developed many varieties—chiefly distinguished by their different flower color (the species plant has magenta blossoms). 'Ingwersen's Variety', named after a noted English horticulturist, is one of the best and has pale pink flowers.

Height: 12 inches to 18 inches
Color: Magenta, rose, pink, white
Bloom Period: Spring
Zones: 3–9
(Pictured on page 142)

Wild Geranium (*G. maculatum*) At the beginning of this century, L. H. Bailey commented that this showy native species should be cultivated more. Today's gardeners are finally heeding this advice. Growing wild throughout much of our country, this easy care perennial sports a profusion of pretty spring flowers. Not quite as neat and tidy as the other geraniums, it is an especially good plant for an informal border.

Height: 18 inches to 24 inches
Color: Blue-violet
Bloom Period: Spring
Zones: 3–9

Bloody Cranesbill (*G. sanguineum*) The popular name for this geranium is derived from its flower color and its beaklike seed heads. Its foliage is somewhat akin to that of the popular candytuft—low-growing, dark green, finely dissected leaves. Small flowers cover this foliage in spring and often sporadically throughout the summer. This is a perfect plant for the front of a partially shaded border (four to five hours of direct sun).

Height: 8 inches to 12 inches
Color: Deep magenta, rose, pink, white
Bloom Period: Late spring and often
                     throughout summer
Zones: 4–8

Lancaster Geranium (*G. sanguineum* var. *striatum*) Horticulturists are still working on the proper botanical name for this wonderful plant. Just look for the name Lancaster, or a Latin variant, and you'll do fine. I grow the Lancaster geranium in both a sunny and a partially shaded setting; it produces a much richer and continuing display of flowers in the former. Even though not so spectacular with less sun, the shaded Lancaster geranium plant still manages to produce a respectable showing of lovely pink flowers for a good two months.

In the bright shade of a mid-May border receiving 3½ hours of full sun, blue Spanish squills nestle next to the emerging rich pink flowers of a clump of bigroot geranium.

Height: 6 inches to 8 inches
Color: Pink
Bloom Period: Late spring to frost
Zones: 4–9
  (Pictured on page 43)

HELLEBORE
Helleborus

There are four very attractive attributes of this genus: the plants bloom in winter, a time when few other perennials do so; they can take dry shade if given a humus-rich soil; they are not bothered by slugs or chewing insects; and they are long-lived. These four factors alone would guarantee hellebores a place in a shade garden. There's more, however: hellebores are good-looking and the flowers last up to three months.

There are an estimated 20 species within the hellebore genus. As shade gardeners become more aware of their ease of care, more of these species will probably be offered commercially. As of now, however, the following are the most readily available hellebores.

Corsican Hellebore *(H. lividus* subsp. *corsicus; often listed and sold as *H. argutifolius.)* Especially recommended for Californian gardens, the pale green flowers of this plant also add a nice early spring accent to eastern flower beds.

Height: 1 foot to 2 feet
Color: Green
Bloom Period: Early spring
Zones: 6–9

Christmas Rose *(H. niger)* A very cold-hardy plant, the Christmas rose will often send up flowering shoots through a layer of snow. Despite its popular name, it generally blooms in late February or early March in colder parts of the country. This plant can be placed in heavily shaded situations.

Height: 10 inches to 18 inches
Color: White
Bloom Period: Winter
Zones: 3–9

Lenten Rose *(H. orientalis)* Taller, not quite so cold-hardy as, and more colorful than the Christmas rose, the Lenten rose starts its three-month bloom period in early March. In my heavily shaded garden the leaves are evergreen and look particularly appealing next to the similarly dark green fronds of the Christmas fern.

Height: 15 inches to 24 inches
Color: White, pink, purple, green
Bloom Period: Early spring
Zones: 4–9

(Pictured on page 98)

DAYLILY

Hemerocallis

The shadier your garden, the less likely it will be that you can grow daylilies. I once moved a clump of a very early golden yellow daylily to a shaded location because I thought the foliage would look well in the spot. What a surprise to see the plant blooming the following year—but what a contrast with the flowers on the mother plant. The mother plant was in an open area receiving about six hours of midday sun; the clump was in an enclosed spot receiving no more than two hours of direct sun. The flowers on the former were numerous and sturdy; the flowers on the latter were few and floppy. In fact, the blooms on the shaded daylily were so wimpy that I cut them off, leaving the spray of foliage as a decorative accent.

If you would like to try some daylilies in a shaded area, consider two approaches. The first is to use short daylilies, perhaps a repeat bloomer such as the popular 'Stella d'Oro'. These should not flop as much as the taller varieties. The second approach would be to use species plants—tough old-timers that are not quite as beautiful as their thousands of hybrid progeny but are sturdier and able to handle drier and darker situations.

Tawny Daylily *(H. fulva)* Naturalized all over the country, this can be seen in woodlands and open fields just about everywhere. There is a double form, variously called 'Kwanso' or 'Flore Pleno', that is not only just as tough but also better-looking. In my garden, the latter does well with only three hours of morning sun and fairly heavy shade the remainder of the day.

Height: 15 inches to 24 inches
Color: Orange
Bloom Period: Summer
Zones: 3–10

Lemon Lily *(H. lilioasphodelus;* sometimes listed and sold as *H. flava.)* The yellow flowers on this old-fashioned stalwart are fragrant and they bloom a week or two before those on the tawny daylily. Try to give this plant at least four hours of direct sun.

Height: 2 feet to 3 feet
Color: Yellow
Bloom Period: Late spring
Zones: 4–10

ALUMROOT
Heuchera

For ease of care, foliage interest, and delicacy of flower, this has to be one of the great shade garden treasures. Native Americans, heucheras are also among the more neglected plants—though recent publicity has brought about increased attention. Coral bells *(H. sanguinea)* are the most popular species; hailing from the bare open spaces of our southwest, they have long been regarded as sun lovers, and this regard has spilled over into opinion about the other members of the genus. It's time for gardeners to rethink their categorization of these plants. Even if they don't flower in a shaded situation, their good-looking foliage is a definite asset in a garden border.

'Dale's Strain' *(H. americana* 'Dale's Strain*')* Found and named by Dale Hendricks of Northcreek Nursery, this shade lover features large leaves mottled with silver markings. In winter the leaves turn purple with the cold and remain fairly evergreen in my garden. Supposedly requiring consistent moisture, the plant has done quite well through several Princeton dry spells. While I have yet to come across enthusiastic praise for the flowers, which are greenish white, miniature versions of those on the more popular coral bells, I think they look rather nice floating about on tall, wiry stems.

Height: 18 inches to 36 inches
Color: Greenish white
Bloom Period: Summer
Zones: 4–9

'Montrose Ruby' *(H. americana* × *H.* 'Palace Purple') This beautiful foliage plant is new in my garden so I cannot vouch for its hardiness. I bought it because of the following description from the Montrose Nursery catalogue: "We were terribly excited when we noticed a flat of heucheras with dark purple leaves, mottled with silver. … Flowers appear in summer rather than spring and are similar to those of *H. villosa.* The best feature of this plant is that it does not lose its dark foliage color even in midsummer."

Height: 1 foot to 2 feet
Color: Creamy white
Bloom Period: Summer
Zones: 4–9

Island Alumroot *(H. maxima)* Recommended for dry shade gardens in central California by the Davis Arboretum, this heuchera cannot survive cold winters. Due to its restricted growing area, this southern California native is not offered by major mail order catalogues but can be obtained at local garden centers in California.

Height: 18 inches to 36 inches
Color: White
Bloom Period: Early spring
Zones: 9–10

'Santa Ana Cardinal' Coral Bells *(H. maxima × H. sanguinea)* Another dry shade garden recommendation by the Davis Arboretum for California gardens, this plant appears to be suitable for Princeton flower beds as well. A hybrid developed by the Rancho Santa Ana Botanic Garden, it features beautiful rose-red flowers that bloom for a long period. Though not available nationwide, I hope that it will soon come to the attention of mail order nurseries.

Height: 18 inches to 36 inches
Color: Rose-red
Bloom Period: Spring through summer
Zones: 7–10

'Palace Purple' *(H. 'Palace Purple')* One of the controversies that horticulturists seem especially prone to is the parentage of plants that seem to pop up out of nowhere. This particular cultivar was first grown in Kew Gardens from seed labeled *Heuchera americana*. While botanists are now fairly confident that the seed was mislabeled, they have yet to agree on a species identification for the plant.

In any case, 'Palace Purple' was named 1991 Plant of the Year by the Perennial Plant Association, selected for its ornamental effect (clouds of long-lasting white flowers swarming above purple-tinged foliage), adaptability to most areas of the United States, minimum maintenance needs, and ease of propagation.

There's a little story connected with that last trait. While easy to grow from seed, 'Palace Purple' does not always produce purple offspring. Since most growers raise the plant from seed, there is a good chance that the foliage on the plant you buy will be a dark green rather than a rich purple. Even so, the plant will still be good-looking and marvelously easy care.

Height: 12 inches to 18 inches
Color: Flowers, white; foliage, purple
to green
Bloom Period: Summer
Zones: 4–8
(Pictured on page 112)

Coral Bells *(H. sanguinea)* A relative newcomer to the garden scene—coral bells were

---

RED-FLOWERED PERENNIALS

Not too many shade plants have red blossoms. The following six, all easy care and described in this chapter, do, enabling gardeners to have a fiery accent from early spring to fall.

EARLY SPRING:
American Columbine *(Aquilegia canadensis)*

SPRING:
Fire Pink *(Silene virginica)*

LATE SPRING INTO SUMMER:
Coral Bells *(Heuchera sanguinea cultivars)*

SUMMER:
Bee Balm *(Monarda didyma)*

LATE SUMMER:
Cardinal Flower *(Lobelia cardinalis)*

FALL:
Virginia Tovara *(T. virginianum 'Variegata')*

only discovered in their native southwest a little over a century ago—these plants quickly became favorites and have remained so to this day. Breeders have developed many cultivars and hybrids with white, pink, or deep scarlet flowers. While I cannot vouch for these plants, I do know that the species will bloom in fairly heavy shade with only three hours of direct sun. The flower stalks, however, flop in such a situation. Still, if that's all the sun you've got, you might want to try this carefree charmer. The slightly variegated foliage clump is attractive and looks well in front of the border.

Height: 12 inches to 18 inches
Color: Red, pink, white
Bloom Period: Spring into summer
Zones: 3–10
(Pictured on page 136)

Hairy Alumroot (*H. villosa*) This reliable and unobtrusive plant needs to be rescued from its relative obscurity. It has deeply lobed, maple-like leaves that form a good-looking foliage clump, one that is not bothered either by slugs or by chewing insects. In summer its slender, wire-thin stems sway with a covering of airy white flowers; these are decorative in arrangements and remain on the plant for well over a month. According to Allan Armitage, this plant is also more at home in humid southern heat than any of the other heucheras. My specimen is called 'Royal Red' and was chosen by Eleanor Saur for the deep purple coloring of its foliage.

Height: 12 inches to 36 inches
Color: White
Bloom Period: Summer
Zones: 5–9

FOAMY BELLS
× *Heucherella*

These are exceptionally lovely shade plant creations, unusual in the garden as well as in their genetic makeup. In 1912, a heuchera hybrid was crossed with *Tiarella cordifolia* and the result was given the official name of *Heucherella*. The plant did not arouse much interest, perhaps because it does best in shaded situations, and these types of garden settings had not yet come into vogue. After World War II, British plantsman Alan Bloom began to cross the two genera and created 'Bridget Bloom' heucherella. This lovely plant is so special that several American nurseries now offer it. I suspect that as American gardens get shadier and as gardeners continue to demand lovely, easy care flowers, there will be more heucherellas offered.

'Bridget Bloom' (*Heucherella*) This wonderful plant has lovely pink flowers closely akin to those of the tiarella; its wiry stems resemble those of the heuchera. The foliage is exquisite—slightly marbled and very neat—and is perfect for the front of the border.

Height: 18 inches
Color: Pink touched with white
Bloom Period: Late spring into summer
Zones: 3–10

CANDYTUFT
Iberis sempervirens

Used for centuries as an edging plant, candytuft is the epitome of easy care. Though it will not bloom profusely in very shady settings, the plant will still feature dark green foliage that provides a handsome edging to a front border.

Height: 9 inches to 12 inches
Color: White
Bloom Period: Spring
Zones: 3–10

IRIS
Iris

There are approximately 200 species of irises and there must be hundreds of cultivars. While the bearded, or German, irises are the best known, these require full sun and are not for the shade garden. The following three will do quite well in shade—preferably the bright shade resulting from highly pruned deciduous trees or from the light bouncing off a bright north-facing wall. While all three prefer moist soil, they are so tough and adaptable that they will also flower in dry situations. And though not totally immune to borers, slugs, and chewing insects, they rarely succumb to them. There's another plus associated with these plants—all have beautiful foliage that adds class to a garden scene long after the flowers have faded.

Crested Iris *(I. cristata)* This diminutive American native brightens up forest floors from Maryland to Georgia, west to Missouri. I think 'Alba', the white form, is the most beautiful of all. It glistens in spring gardens.

Height: 4 inches to 9 inches
Color: Lilac, blue, white, purple
Bloom Period: Spring
Zones: 4–9
(Pictured on page 43)

Yellow Flag *(I. pseudacorus)* This ancient and beautiful plant has just recently enjoyed a renaissance in garden popularity. Though its bright yellow flowers are eye-catching, it is chiefly grown for its tall sprays of swordlike foliage. This plant has long been one of my favorites.

Height: 2 feet to 6 feet
Color: Yellow

Bloom Period: Late spring
Zones: 4–9
(Foliage pictured on page 158)

Siberian Iris *(I. sibirica)* Native to moist meadows, this widely offered and photographed plant bears lustrous flowers that are a standout in late spring gardens.

Height: 2 feet to 4 feet
Color: White, blue, purple
Bloom Period: Late spring
Zones: 4–10

LOBELIA
Lobelia

Lobelias were among the first New World plants shipped to England. There they have long been admired for their late summer bloom and their ease of care. American gardeners are finally coming to appreciate their many qualities, not least of which is that they are perfect for shade gardens.

Cardinal Flower *(L. cardinalis)* Supposedly named by King Charles I's wife because the brilliant red flowers reminded her of a cardinal's stockings, these water-loving plants can grow in quite heavy shade. They are short-lived but will reseed readily in moist situations.

Height: 2 feet to 4 feet
Color: Scarlet
Bloom Period: Late summer
Zones: 2–9

Hybrid Lobelias *(L. × hybrida)* These disease- and pest-resistant flowers are the work of breeders in the U.S., Canada, and England. They bear spikes of flowers that swirl through

The purples, reds, and violets of Thurman Maness's hybrid lobelias create a colorful late August tapestry at the Leonard J. Buck Garden in Far Hills, New Jersey.

the red-blue-white color spectrum. Even the foliage has not been immune to horticultural tinkering; plants have been developed with bronze, mahogany, or dark red leaves. These new lobelias exhibit all the vigor associated with hybrids: they bloom longer and can take both drier and colder situations than their parents (chiefly *L. cardinalis* and *L. siphilitica*).

Thurman Maness of The Wildwood Flower (see address in Appendix) is one of the premier lobelia hybrid creators in our country. 'Ruby Slippers' is his claim to fame. It is a magnificent plant, with rich ruby red flowers and a bloom period that extends over two months. Maness has developed many other lobelias as

well, plants in lavenders, blues, and even multicolors.

Height: 2 feet to 5 feet
Color: The entire red-blue-white spectrum
Bloom Period: Various times from July through September
Zones: 4–9

Big Blue Lobelia (*L. siphilitica*) In a classic con job, American Indians convinced early settlers that this plant cured syphilis. It was, of course, immediately sent back to Europe where it received its unfortunate botanical name. This is an exceptionally tough plant, one called a weed by some and easy care by others. To keep unwanted seedlings to a minimum, cut off the flower stalks as they set seed. This action has the further beneficial result of encouraging flowering side shoots. I like the white form, which blooms a long time and looks quite handsome in my late summer garden.

Height: 2 feet to 4 feet
Color: Blue, white
Bloom Period: Late summer into fall
Zones: 4–9
(Pictured on page 116)

VIRGINIA BLUEBELLS
Mertensia virginica

Native throughout the eastern half of our country, these lovely woodland flowers are a spring delight. Since their foliage goes dormant by late spring, they are especially good candidates for spots eventually covered by emerging hosta leaves.

Height: 1 foot to 2 feet
Color: Pink buds opening to sky-blue flowers
Bloom Period: Early spring
Zones: 3–9

ALLEGHENY MONKEY FLOWER

Mimulus ringens

This is another long-blooming, easy care woodland native that is sure to become more popular. I planted two, about three feet apart, in a brightly shaded border filled with rich humus and close to a hose so that these moisture-loving plants could be watered easily and frequently. Despite their being so close together, one plant received one hour of direct sun and the other, three; the former had only one blossom throughout the summer and the latter was covered with a continuous supply of flowers for over two months.

Height: 2 feet to 3 feet
Color: Purple splotched with yellow
Bloom Period: All summer
Zones: 3–9

BEE BALM

Monarda didyma

Although this plant will flower in darkly shaded areas receiving as little as two hours of direct sun, it prefers sunnier situations. Having a mind of its own, it will march forward to a more congenial setting. Even in pleasant surroundings it tends to spread rapidly. Keep your eye on this plant not only to see it stays within bounds but also to watch the hummingbirds attracted to its flowers, particularly to the red ones. In warm, humid climates the foliage is often covered with mildew. When that happens, I simply cut the plant to the ground; this drastic action has never affected the following year's performance.

Height: 18 inches to 40 inches
Color: Red, white, pink, purple
Bloom Period: Summer

Blooming continuously for 2 months in a bright shade border receiving just 3 hours of direct sun, Allegheny monkey flower is a long-neglected American native.

Zones: 4–9
(Pictured on page 136)

SUNDROPS

Oenothera fruticosa; often listed and sold as *O. tetragona* or *O. youngii*

Though this tough American native is usually recommended for sunny situations, I have seen it blooming away in a circle of bright shade at the base of a tree. Japanese beetles usually emerge to eat the foliage just as the last bright yellow blossom falls to the ground. My easy care solution is to take away the food source; that is, to cut the foliage to its basal rosette. Even with such a stern measure, the sundrops will spread through underground runners. These are easily uprooted if they stray into forbidden areas.

Height: 18 inches to 30 inches
Color: Yellow
Bloom Period: Summer
Zones: 4–9

BEARD TONGUE
Penstemon smallii

"This is the best eastern native penstemon for the woodland garden," says Ken Moore, assistant director of the North Carolina Botanical Garden. Noting the dramatic beauty of the plant's vertical spires of pink and white flowers, Moore goes on to say that "fine gravel is a good mulch material to scatter around the base of the plant to protect against fungus problems during warm humid periods." Generally a short-lived perennial, beard tongue will self-seed in bare soil patches. Exposing the basal foliage of the plant to winter sunlight helps to prolong its life.

Height: 18 inches to 24 inches
Color: Pink and white
Bloom Period: Late spring
Zones: 4–10
   (Pictured on page 63)

PHLOX

Two perennial members of the diverse phlox genus are shade garden standouts. Both grow on their own in woodlands throughout the eastern half of the U.S. That says something about their maintenance needs: just give them humus-rich soil and then leave them alone. The blue woodland phlox will spread by runners and will cover a woodland floor with its fragrant blue flowers in spring. The old garden phlox is considerably taller and blooms for an extended period starting in August.

Blue Woodland Phlox *(P. divaricata)* This is a great transition flower in the spring garden, coming into its own as the last daffodils fade, and lingering long enough to greet the white of the candytuft. Keep cutting the fragrant flowers for indoor arrangements and the plant will keep blooming outdoors. Rabbits are supposed to love this phlox; if such animals are in your area, you will probably not be able to grow it. Since the plant goes dormant during Princeton's dry summer heat, I keep it in the middle of the border so that plants in front will cover up any bare spots.

Height: 9 inches to 15 inches
Color: Light blue
Bloom Period: Spring
Zones: 4–9
   (Pictured on page 59)

Old Garden Phlox *(P. paniculata)* I confess to falling victim to the tyranny of taste. Having read universal condemnations of the ugliness of this wild plant's magenta flowers (generally, only fancy cultivars are now offered), I never wrote how much I liked it, how my plants were actually a pleasing pale purple or a bright white, how they did not need staking, and how they bloomed prolifically in heavy shade with only two to three hours of direct sun. And then, bless his gardener's heart, Allen Lacy wrote an August 1990 *New York Times* article that legitimized this plant by proclaiming its beauty, its resistance to mildew and spider mite (I keep both at bay by cutting selected stems to the ground, thus thinning out each clump and ensuring lots of air circulation), and its extended late summer bloom.

Height: 2 feet to 5 feet
Color: Magenta, white
Bloom Period: Late summer into fall
Zones: 4–9
  (Pictured on page 116)

JACOB'S LADDER
Polemonium
With dark green foliage resembling that of the Christmas fern and pretty flowers in the first part of the garden year, polemoniums are wonderful plants for the front of a brightly shaded border. Though not as widely known, our native Jacob's ladder is a much tougher plant—particularly with regard to summer humidity—than the European polemonium.

European Jacob's Ladder (*P. caeruleum*) This is a favorite overseas and was among the first European plants brought to the U.S. European breeders have taken a renewed interest in it and have recently announced the introduction of an apricot-colored flower.

Height: 12 inches to 36 inches
Color: Blue, white, apricot
Bloom Period: Late spring
Zones: 2–7

American Jacob's Ladder (*P. reptans*) This is one of my favorite plants, blooming profusely for up to six weeks starting in early April. Its flowers are lovely in arrangements, long-lasting and slowly turning to a delicate white. It is also a great container plant for shaded balconies or terraces.

Height: 8 inches to 20 inches
Color: Blue
Bloom Period: Spring
Zones: 3–8
  (Pictured on pages 27 and 80)

PRIMROSE
Primula
These beautiful, brightly colored spring flowers are a staple in British and Japanese shade gardens. Most have a hard time in the humid heat blanketing much of the U.S.; those that do survive require a great deal of ground moisture. Placed in the right setting, the following three are easy care and definitely worth trying.

Japanese Primrose (*P. japonica*) At Henry Francis du Pont's Winterthur estate, the Japanese primroses are planted in the ideal easy care situation: along a brightly shaded stream bank. Often called candelabra primroses, these feature rounded pompons of multicolored flowers on slender stalks.

Height: 1 foot to 2 feet
Color: Crimson, pink, white
Bloom Period: Late spring
Zones: 5–8

Sieboldi Primrose (*P. sieboldii*) Harold Epstein, President Emeritus of the American Rock Garden Society, has written that this primrose is the best for American gardens. When attacked by spider mite or stressed by summer humidity, the plant retreats—the foliage goes dormant and the roots hide underground. This is the only primrose with such an effective defense mechanism.

Height: 6 inches to 15 inches
Color: Purple, mauve, rose, pink, white
Bloom Period: Spring
Zones: 4–9
  (Pictured on page 59)

English Primrose (*P. vulgaris*) I love the cheery yellow of this British wildflower, and so did Thomas Jefferson, who grew it at Monticello.

Withstanding more shade than other primroses, it has no trouble surviving (and reseeding itself) hot, humid Princeton summers. Though not as elegant as the Japanese or sieboldi primroses, it is probably the most easy care.

Height: 6 inches
Color: Pale yellow
Bloom Period: Spring
Zones: 5–8

LUNGWORT
Pulmonaria saccharata

This is a bright to heavy shade plant that provides something of interest throughout the growing season: it is covered with lovely blue flowers in spring and then boasts foliage splashed with gray. For a while I thought it was perfect, but then Princeton went through an extremely hot, dry spring and the leaves became covered with mildew. Over a period of two or three weeks, I cut and discarded the foliage and watered frequently. These actions eliminated the mildew. I prefer the 'Mrs. Moon' cultivar, while the Boerner Botanical Gardens in Wisconsin recommends 'Margery Fish'.

Height: 9 inches to 18 inches
Color: Buds, pink; flowers, blue; foliage,
        green, mottled and splashed with gray
Bloom Period: Spring
Zones: 3–9
(Pictured on page 27)

CONEFLOWER
Rudbeckia

These gaily colored American natives are usually recommended for sunny borders. The following two, however, do quite well in shade.

Black-eyed Susan (*R. fulgida*) This plant actually requires the cooling influence of shade

in order to bloom better. A true perennial, it spreads primarily through underground runners and is not subject to mildew the way the similarly named black-eyed Susan *R. hirta* is (this last, a self-seeding annual or biennial, is often seen in sunny fields along highways). The 'Goldsturm' cultivar, rather than the species *R. fulgida*, is most often offered at garden centers. In my garden this plant flowers profusely with just three hours of direct sun in a rather heavily shaded spot.

Height: 18 inches to 30 inches
Color: Golden yellow with black centers
Bloom Period: Late summer
Zones: 3–10

Green Coneflower (*R. laciniata*) Ken Moore, assistant director of the North Carolina Botanical Garden, recommends this yellow-flowered perennial for the brilliant color it adds to the deepest of shady gardens in late summer and early fall. "It is well suited to a naturally moist area," he says, "but can be maintained in better drained sites, where it is not as aggressive as in moister conditions." The variety *hortensia* has double flowers and is usually sold as 'Golden Glow'.

Height: 30 inches to 72 inches
Color: Yellow
Bloom Period: Late summer to fall
Zones: 3–9

BLOODROOT
Sanguinaria canadensis

There is a stately elegance about this American native. Its brilliant white petals gleam above the brown earth of early spring; double forms—called either 'Multiplex' or 'Flore Pleno'—are even more spectacular. Gardeners with beds heavily shaded by deciduous trees also value the beauty of the bloodroot foliage, which pairs well with that of hostas, fernleaf corydalis, and astilbes. If not watered during dry periods, however, bloodroot foliage will go dormant (without any detriment to the next year's flowers). Where open ground is available, this plant will seed itself. "Once established," according to Ken Moore, assistant director of the North Carolina Botanical Garden, "the seedlings will eventually display a wide variety of flower forms."

Height: 6 inches to 9 inches
Color: White
Bloom Period: Early spring
Zones: 3–9

SHOWY STONECROP
Sedum spectabile

While usually recommended for sunny settings, this old-fashioned fall bloomer does quite well with only four hours of direct sun in my garden. Bees love its flat tops of bright pink flowers and hover about them constantly.

Height: 18 inches to 24 inches
Color: Pink
Bloom Period: Late summer into fall
Zones: 4–10

FIRE PINK
Silene virginica

Native to open woods and rocky hills from New Jersey to Minnesota, south to Georgia and Oklahoma, this is one of the few red-flowered shade perennials. "The secret to maintaining this plant several years or more," advises Ken Moore, assistant director of the North Carolina Botanical Garden, "is to take care that the basal foliage is not covered by fallen leaves during winter months." Moore also notes that fire pink will self-sow easily on exposed grounds.

Height: 18 inches to 24 inches
Color: Red
Bloom Period: Spring
Zones: 3–9

LAMB'S EARS
Stachys byzantina; also listed and sold as
S. lanata or *S. olympica*

This is an old-fashioned favorite, long grown and admired in British gardens. It has soft, furry gray leaves that are fun to pet and that add a nice contrast to the garden scene. Though it is generally recommended for sunny settings, I have had great success using lamb's ears as an edging plant in a shade border, one receiv-

Fire pink blazes away at Pennsylvania's Bowman's Hill Wildflower Preserve on a mid-May morning.

SUMMER-FLOWERING PERENNIALS

The following plants are in peak bloom during the months of July and August.

Common Monkshood (*Aconitum napellus*)
False Anemone (*Anemonopsis macrophylla*)
Black Cohosh (*Cimicifuga racemosa*)
Yellow Corydalis (*C. lutea*)
Hollow Joe-Pye Weed (*Eupatorium fistulosum*)
False Baby's Breath (*Galium mollugo* 'Victor Jones')
Lancaster Geranium (*G. sanguineum* var. striatum)

Tawny Daylily (*Hemerocallis fulva*)
'Palace Purple' (*Heuchera* 'Palace Purple')
Hairy Alumroot (*Heuchera villosa*)
Ligularia (*L. przewalskii, L.* 'The Rocket')
Cardinal Flower (*Lobelia cardinalis*)
Hybrid Lobelias (*L.* × *hybrida*)
Allegheny Monkey Flower (*Mimulus ringens*)
Bee Balm (*Monarda didyma*)

ing about three hours of direct sun, and heavy shade the remainder of the day.

Height: 12 inches to 18 inches
Color: Flowers, purple; foliage, silver gray
Bloom Period: Summer
Zones: 4–9

CELANDINE POPPY
Stylophorum diphyllum

The yellow flowers on this native perennial match those of the daffodil in size and cheeriness. Unlike daffodils, however, this plant will keep on producing flowers for almost two months.

Height: 12 inches to 18 inches
Color: Yellow
Bloom Period: Spring into early summer
Zones: 4–9
(Pictured on page 80 and right.)

FOAMFLOWER
Tiarella

Native to the woodlands of North America and East Asia, foamflowers are small delightful plants with fluffy flower spikes. Easily grown in full to part shade, they do require soil rich in organic matter—the kind of setting in which they flourish naturally in the wild. The fast-spreading Allegheny foamflower (*T. cordifolia*) is generally regarded as a groundcover; it

The bright yellow flowers of celandine poppies bloom for almost 2 months, starting in mid-April.

FALL-FLOWERING PERENNIALS

The following plants are in peak bloom after Labor Day.

Japanese Anemone (*A. hupehensis, A. ×
    hybrida, A. tomentosa* 'Robustissima')
Aster (*A. divaricatus, A. ericoides, A. novae-
    angliae* 'Harrington's Pink')
Hardy Begonia (*B. grandis*)
Bugbane (*Cimicifuga simplex* 'The Pearl')
Boneset (*Eupatorium coelestinum, E. pur-
    pureum, E. rugosum*)
Yellow Waxbells (*Kirengeshoma palmata*)

Hybrid Lobelias (*L. × hybrida*)
Big Blue Lobelia (*L. siphilitica*)
Old Garden Phlox (*P. paniculata*)
Black-eyed Susan (*Rudbeckia fulgida*)
Green Coneflower (*Rudbeckia laciniata*)
Canadian Burnet (*Sanguisorba canadensis*)
Goldenrod (*Solidago caesia, S. sphacelata*)
Virginia Tovara (*T. virginianum* 'Variegata')
Toad Lily (*Tricyrtis formosana, T. hirta*)

is described in Chapter 6. The two plants listed here slowly form clumps, which may be divided after several years.

Height: 6 inches to 12 inches
Color: Pale pink, white
Bloom Period: Spring
Zones: 3–9

Pink Foamflower (*T. cordifolia* var. *wherryi;* also listed and sold as *T. cordifolia* var. *collina* and *T. wherryi.*) This native was discovered by noted American horticulturist Dr. Edgar T. Wherry. It forms a delicate clump of good-looking foliage and sends up spikes of cotton candy cones of pink flowers in spring. As has happened with so many of our native plants, the flower was neglected here and honored abroad. In 1939, seeds were sent to England, where it became known as "an invaluable plant for half-open woodland . . . a shade lover . . . [of]. . . charm and beauty." In 1948 this plant received a Royal Horticultural Society Award of Merit. At that time the only way Americans could obtain this flower commercially was to import it from England! Happily, this situation has changed drastically in recent years and the pink foamflower is now offered by several American nurseries.

Blue sprays of bugloss and feathery flowers of pink foamflower add colorful charm to a shade border in May. The foliage of variegated hosta fills the background of this setting.

Japanese Foamflower *(T. polyphylla)* This is a tiny plant, one that I think rock gardeners would be particularly enchanted with. It has delicate white flowers that bloom on slender stems. The veins on the hairy, rounded leaves often have a maroonish cast.

Height: 10 inches to 18 inches
Color: Creamy white
Bloom Period: Spring
Zones: Not fully established. I grow it in zone 6 and believe it should be fine in zones 4–8.

VIRGINIA TOVARA

T. virginianum 'Variegata'; recently put with *Polygonums* and reclassified as *Persicaria*

Linda Yang introduced me to this wonderful shade plant, which has just started to be offered commercially. It has creamy white and soft green variegated foliage throughout all of summer and then produces tiny red flowers on wiry stems in September. I have it in a bright shade setting that receives three hours of direct sun and about an hour or more of dappled sun. Given its ease of care and bright good looks, this could be one of the up-and-coming shade plants of the nineties.

Height: 2 feet to 4 feet
Color: Flower, red; foliage, cream-splashed green
Bloom Period: Late summer into fall
Zones: 4–8

SPIDERWORT

Tradescantia × andersoniana; sometimes listed and sold as *T. virginiana*

I grow this plant in a dry, deeply shaded setting that receives about two hours of direct morning sun. In this place it will bear its dark blue flowers at the end of its straplike foliage for a good month or so starting in late spring. It does not spread here as these plants do in sunnier situations.

Height: 12 inches to 36 inches
Color: Blue, rose, white
Bloom Period: Spring
Zones: 4–9

ADDITIONAL SHADE PERENNIALS TO CONSIDER

The following perennials are not included in the selection recommended above because I have not had sufficient experience with them or because I have had problems with them. Since all are highly praised by others, you may want to try one or more.

COMMON MONKSHOOD

Aconitum napellus

The easy care shade gardener's equivalent of delphiniums, monkshoods bear lovely blue flowers on erect stems in cool, moist, brightly shaded settings. Be aware, however, that the entire plant is extremely poisonous.

Height: 3 feet to 4 feet
Color: Blue
Bloom Period: Summer
Zones: 3–8
(Pictured on page 116)

PHEASANT'S-EYE
Adonis amurensis

These cheery yellow flowers are among the first perennials to bloom, usually appearing just as the last of the snowdrop flowers open and joining the blues of squills. Unlike the early bulbs, pheasant's-eye has an attractive, ferny foliage.

Height: 9 inches to 15 inches
Color: Yellow
Bloom Period: Late winter
Zones: 4–8

SPIKENARD
Aralia racemosa

Recommended by Bowman's Hill Wildflower Preserve, this native American perennial has a shrublike appearance. Its foliage provides a nice backdrop to other plantings; in the fall it is covered with beautiful berries.

Height: 4 feet to 6 feet
Color: Flowers, white; berries, deep purple
Bloom Period: Summer
Zones: 4–8

MARSH MARIGOLD
Caltha palustris

This is a lovely native plant that I have never grown and probably never will, because I do not have a bog garden or marshy soil. Should such conditions exist on your property, you would definitely want to have this splendid, easy care flower.

Height: 12 inches to 20 inches
Color: Yellow
Bloom Period: Early spring
Zones: 3–9

BLUE COHOSH
Caulophyllum thalictroides

A long neglected American native, this plant was recommended by L. H. Bailey at the beginning of this century because of its attractive appearance, trim growth, and interesting habit. Found in deep woods from New Brunswick to South Carolina and Missouri, it is especially suitable for dark areas.

Height: 12 inches to 14 inches
Color: Flowers, yellow-green; berries, rich blue
Bloom Period: Spring
Zones: 4–8

SHOOTING STAR
Dodecatheon meadia

A dainty little flower for the spring garden, this is an old-fashioned woodland plant not often seen today.

Height: 6 inches to 20 inches
Color: White, purple, lavender, deep rose
Bloom Period: Spring
Zones: 4–9

BOWMAN'S ROOT
Gillenia trifoliata

I have seen some very attractive pictures of this perennial. They always show a large number of white starlike flowers covering the plant in midsummer. Unfortunately, bowman's root is having a hard time surviving in my garden. In the two years that I have had it in my borders, it has barely managed to produce a main shoot. Obviously, this is not an easy care success for all shade gardeners!

Height: 2 feet to 4 feet
Color: White

Bloom Period: **Summer**
Zones: **4–8**

ROUND-LOBED HEPATICA

H. americana

An excellent plant for a dry woodland garden, this native American plant grows wild over a great geographical expanse—from Nova Scotia to Manitoba, south to Florida and Missouri—and is an easy care recommendation of the Abraham Lincoln Memorial Garden in Springfield, Illinois. I grow the sharp-lobed hepatica (*H. acutiloba*), which has pointier leaves. Some botanists think the two are different forms of the same species. Both are charming in early spring.

Height: **6 inches**
Color: **Pale lilac, pinkish white**
Bloom Period: **Early spring**
Zones: **4–8**

Orange-yellow flowers of bigleaf ligularia and spraying foliage of yellow flag iris create a peaceful mood on a hot late August morning at the Leonard J. Buck Garden in Far Hills, New Jersey.

TWINLEAF

Jeffersonia diphylla

Named in 1792 by noted American horticulturist Benjamin S. Barton in honor of his friend Thomas Jefferson, the white flowers of this spring native bloom around Jefferson's early April birthday. There is a lovely planting of this flower in a shaded oval bed at Monticello. In my garden, however, the plant has struggled to survive and, after three years, has yet to bloom.

Height: **10 inches to 12 inches**
Color: **White**
Bloom Period: **Spring**
Zones: **5–8**

YELLOW WAXBELLS

Kirengeshoma palmata

I have mixed emotions about this late-blooming shade perennial, and I believe that Princeton's summer heat and humidity have something to do with these feelings. As summer progresses, the plant's maplelike leaves turn ugly with brown and gray splotches. One year, however, we had an exceptionally rainy and rather cool summer season. Under those conditions, this plant was magnificent, and its waxy, pale yellow bell-shaped flowers bloomed exquisitely for well over a month.

Height: **3 feet to 4 feet**
Color: **Pale yellow**
Bloom Period: **Late summer**
Zones: **5–8**

LIGULARIA

Ligularia

New to gardens in the twentieth century, ligularias crave moisture and afternoon shade and tend to wilt in hot humidity. They are not, therefore, for all shade gardens, but can be quite dramatic in some. They bloom in mid- to late summer—a time when most shade perennials are too tired to perform. Slugs will devour seedlings; established plants simply grow too fast to be bothered by these pests.

There is much confusion between Shavalski's ligularia and 'The Rocket'. Plants bought through nurseries or the mail are often mislabeled and could be either one. The four-lined plant bug likes both; should you spot a profusion of brown spots on the foliage, dust once or twice with rotenone.

Bigleaf Ligularia (*L. dentata*) Grown chiefly for its large heart-shaped leaves, this accent plant also sports orange daisylike flowers in late summer. The cultivar 'Desdemona' is prized because it is shorter than the species plant, withstands summer heat better than most other ligularias, and has purple on its leaf undersides.

Height: 3 feet to 4 feet
Color: Orange, orange-yellow
Bloom Period: Late summer
Zones: 4–8

Shavalski's Ligularia (*L. przewalskii*) The foliage on this plant looks like black-edged maple leaves. The yellow flowers on long spikes are dramatic in arrangements.

Height: 5 feet to 6 feet
Color: Yellow
Bloom Period: Summer
Zones: 4–8

'The Rocket' (*L. 'The Rocket'*) Developed by Alan Bloom in England, this is a shorter version of Shivalski's ligularia.

Height: 18 inches to 24 inches
Color: Yellow
Bloom Period: Summer
Zones: 4–8

(Pictured on pages 21 and 25)

MITERWORT
Mitella diphylla

With small lacy flowers on a short spike, this native can be found in spring woodlands throughout a large area, one encompassing Quebec, Ontario, Minnesota, Missouri, Alabama, and Virginia. It is an unassuming plant that possesses a quiet charm.

Height: 12 inches to 18 inches
Color: White
Bloom Period: Spring
Zones: 3–8

POKEWEED
Phytolacca americana

I am very fond of saying that one person's easy care perennial is another person's weed; this is certainly the case with pokeweed. Recommended by Gary B. Parrot, grounds manager at Michigan State University, and warmly praised by Allen Lacy in his book *The Garden in Autumn*, this ubiquitous perennial grows in sun or shade from Maine to Florida and west to Mexico. Its succulent-like, warm green foliage starts to take off in early summer and reaches statuesque proportions by fall. It bears dripping white flowers which turn into beautiful black-purple berries. I think it an obnoxious weed, one that I am constantly digging out of my borders.

Height: 4 feet to 7 feet
Color: Flowers, white;
        berries, black-purple
Bloom Period: Summer
Zones: 3–9

SOLOMON'S SEAL
Polygonatum

Though I have no personal experience with either of the following native plants, they are highly recommended by others as being low-maintenance perennials for heavily shaded areas.

Giant Solomon's Seal *(P. commutatum)* A popular woodland flower, this has handsome arching stems and is grown chiefly as a foliage accent in the garden border.

Height: 3 feet to 7 feet
Color: White
Bloom Period: Late spring
Zones: 4–9

Small Solomon's Seal *(P. pubescens)* Heather McCargo of Garden in the Woods recommends this spring native, which grows wild from Nova Scotia to Manitoba and then cuts a southern path through Indiana down to Georgia. Rarely offered in commercial trade, seeds can be obtained from Garden in the Woods.

Height: 1 foot to 3 feet
Color: Flowers, white; berries, blue
Bloom Period: Spring
Zones: 4–9

CANADIAN BURNET
Sanguisorba canadensis

Recommended by the U.S. National Arboretum as a fall shade perennial, this good-looking plant is native from Labrador to Michigan south to Georgia. Its bottlebrush flowers are quite attractive in a late summer garden.

Height: 4 feet to 6 feet
Color: White
Bloom Period: Late summer into fall
Zones: 3–8

FALSE SOLOMON'S SEAL
Smilacina racemosa

This lovely native has plumes of white flowers

in spring. It is attractive in the formal setting of Henry Francis du Pont's estate at Winterthur as well as in Gay Bumgarner's woodland garden in Missouri. Its natural range covers an area bounded by Quebec, Tennessee, Arizona, and Virginia. Notice how it sidesteps the extreme humidity of the southeast; in such areas, extra—but not excessive—care is needed to grow the plant.

Height: 18 inches to 36 inches
Color: White
Bloom Period: Spring
Zones: 3–8

GOLDENROD
Solidago

For years Americans have admired the beauty of goldenrods in fall fields, and the British have treasured them in fall flower borders. Now garden books and magazine articles are spreading the message that goldenrods should be honored in their home country. They are not elegant plants, however, and are best placed in informal borders. While most goldenrods do best in sun, the following two can be grown in shade.

Wreath Goldenrod *(S. caesia)* Tom Stevenson, plant propagator at Bowman's Hill Wildflower Preserve, highly recommends this low-growing woodland goldenrod. It certainly is an adaptable one, growing wild from Nova Scotia to Wisconsin, south to Florida and Texas.

Height: 1 foot to 3 feet
Color: Yellow
Bloom Period: Late summer
Zones: 4–9

False Goldenrod *(S. sphacelata)* The 'Golden Fleece' cultivar of this plant has become quite popular in recent years. I have the species goldenrod and have not been all that impressed with its appearance in flower borders, though it certainly is easy care. By chance, however, this prolific self-seeder popped up in the midst of an ivy-and-periwinkle spot under a fir tree. There it actually looks quite nice and adds a touch of yellow to a dry shady spot that is normally just green in fall.

Height: 12 inches to 36 inches
Color: Yellow
Bloom Period: Fall
Zones: 3–8

TOAD LILY
Tricyrtis

The unusual orchidlike flowers in this genus are valued for their oddity as well as for their fall bloom.

Formosa Toad Lily *(T. formosana)* Allan Armitage highly recommends this plant for its flower size, color, and six-week-long bloom period.

Height: 12 inches to 36 inches
Color: Mauve
Bloom Period: Fall
Zones: 4–9

Common Toad Lily *(T. hirta)* This is the most widely available toad lily. Its freckle-faced flowers—white, heavily splotched with purple—are hard to miss in the garden.

Height: 12 inches to 36 inches
Color: Lilac, white
Bloom Period: Late summer into fall
Zones: 4–9

BIG MERRYBELLS
Uvularia grandiflora

The primary reason this plant is not in the recommended list is because slugs slurp on it mercilessly in my garden. In the wild, this

The bright yellow flowers of big merrybells bloom at the same time as Virginia bluebells in spring.

charming spring native can be found in woods from Quebec to North Dakota, south to Georgia and Oklahoma. When not mangled by slugs, it bears good-looking foliage and lovely drooping, bell-shaped yellow flowers.

Height: 12 inches to 30 inches
Color: Yellow
Bloom Period: Spring
Zones: 3–9

SOURCES: Unless noted otherwise in an individual description, the plants can all be obtained from one or more of the following mail order firms: Bluestone Perennials, Crownsville Nursery, Forestfarm, Holbrook Farm, Native Gardens, Primrose Path, and White Flower Farm. Addresses for these firms are presented in the Appendix.

FOR FURTHER INFORMATION on perennials, two reference works are essential. These are *Herbaceous Perennial Plants* by Allan M. Armitage and *Perennials for American Gardens* by Ruth Rogers Clausen and Nicolas H. Ekstrom.

MAIL ORDER FIRMS

Local garden centers simply do not have room to stock all the great wealth of plant material available to gardeners today. Thus, acquisitive gardeners—those who like to experiment with many different kinds of flowers—inevitably come to rely on mail order nurseries.

One of my pet peeves is to read a garden book filled with descriptions of many wonderful flowers and then to turn to the back and find 20 or more firms listed as sources. I have neither the time to order from, nor the patience to read through, 20 different catalogues. To simplify matters for readers of this book, I have deliberately limited the number of sources.

In addition to the bulb merchants listed for plants described as bulbs, corms, or tubers, and the seed sellers for plants described as annuals or biennials, I refer to a core list of only seven nurseries for all remaining shade flowers. Using just these seven, you can track down about 95 percent of the plants discussed in this book. For the remaining 5 percent, I have indicated specific sources (for example, The Wildwood Flower for the 'Ruby Slippers' hybrid lobelia); these firms are reviewed in the supplemental list on page 166.

While I have dealt with all the core nurseries described below and can personally recommend them, I would like to emphasize that there are many other fine establishments that do a wonderful job in searching out new plants and bringing them to the public's attention. If I limited myself to just the firms listed here, I would be missing out on many new plant introductions.

I try to order from at least one new nursery each year, and I encourage readers of this book to do the same.

The following sample is deliberately representative of the kinds of different mail order firms; that is, it includes large nationally known firms and small businesses with special gardening niches. *The smaller nurseries do not have the resources to offer free catalogues; where a price is indicated, a check must accompany the catalogue request.*

BULB MERCHANTS

THE DAFFODIL MART
Route 3, Box 794
Gloucester, Virginia 23061
(804) 693–3966

Primarily a wholesale firm, The Daffodil Mart offers a huge selection of bulbs, many of them extremely difficult to find, at very low prices. Is there a catch? Well, yes. You have to order in bulk: prices are usually quoted per 100 bulbs. The best way to take advantage of the selection and prices offered by this firm is to team up with friends and send in a joint order.

MCCLURE & ZIMMERMAN
108 West Winnebago Street
P.O. Box 368
Friesland, Wisconsin 53935
(414) 326–4220

It's hard to resist the informative descriptions in the catalogue offered by these bulb merchants. In addition to a large selection of daffodils and hybrid tulips, they offer a solid list of species tulips and many of the lesser known bulbs.

SMITH & HAWKEN
25 Corte Madera
Mill Valley, California 94941
(415) 383–2000

Smith & Hawken is usually associated with the gracious living, in an environmentally correct manner, of course, that is accompanied by lovely teak benches, wide-brimmed straw hats, and good, solid English garden tools. The firm also puts out a beautifully illustrated bulb catalogue. Not very well known is that its prices are among the lowest offered by retail suppliers. The quality is superb and the selection quite good.

WHITE FLOWER FARM
Litchfield, Connecticut 06759–0050
(203) 496–9600

Usually associated with, and rightly praised for its championship of, herbaceous perennials, White Flower Farm has expanded its offerings in recent years to include a solid list of bulbs.

COMMERCIAL SEED SOURCES

The following firms all offer the basic shade flowers, such as impatiens and begonias, as well as a wide variety of sun flowers and vegetables. Each firm has a distinct personality and offers at least one or two plants not available elsewhere.

W. ATLEE BURPEE & CO.
300 Park Avenue
Warminster, Pennsylvania PA 18974
(215) 674–9633

One of the most prominent American seed companies, Burpee offers a wide range (many of them flowers that the company itself has developed) of dependable annuals, biennials,

and perennials. In recent years, the firm has added bulbs and garden-ready bedding plants to its offerings.

DEGIORGI SEED COMPANY
6011 "N" Street
Omaha, Nebraska 68117
(402) 731–3901
Catalogue Price: $2.00

In business since the beginning of this century, DeGiorgi offers a large selection of annuals, biennials, and perennials—many of them good old-fashioned varieties. The company declares that it seeks to provide "big variety, good value, plus [an] easy to read and informative catalogue format."

HARRIS SEEDS
60 Saginaw Drive
P.O. Box 22960
Rochester, New York 14692–2960
(716) 442–0410

Another old-timer (the firm began operation in 1879), Harris Seeds offers a broad selection of flowers, with new varieties continually being added. Flowers the firm deems as exceptionally good performers are marked with a special designation in the catalogue.

PARK SEED COMPANY
Cokesbury Road
Greenwood, South Carolina 29647–0001
(803) 223–7333

The oldest and largest family-owned mail order seed company in the U.S., Park offers an excellent selection of annuals, biennials, and perennials. It is known for its exclusives and introductions—beautiful plants that are soon afterward offered by the competition. Bulbs and plants are also featured in its luxuriously illustrated catalogue.

PINETREE GARDEN SEEDS
New Gloucester, Maine 04260
(207) 926–3400

Founded in 1979, this firm specializes in providing seed for the home gardener with less space and, thus, less need for large seed packets. It offers an interesting selection of seed for flowers (several rarely offered by other firms), plus tools, gadgets, and the most extensive offering of garden books by any seed or nursery firm.

STOKES SEEDS INC.
Box 548
Buffalo, New York 14240
(416) 688–4300

Primarily a wholesaler, selling seed to 38,000 large commercial growers in the Northeast and Canada, Stokes also makes its catalogue available to over 300,000 smaller growers, roadside stand operators, and serious gardeners. The packaged seeds for its superb selection of flowers are offered in packet size (generally 50 to 100 seeds) and then by measured weight (1/16 ounce up to 8 ounces).

THOMPSON & MORGAN INC.
P.O. Box 1308
Jackson, New Jersey 08527
(908) 363–2225

Each year this giant among seed companies distributes its "most comprehensive illustrated seed catalogue in the world" to almost 2 million gardeners. In business for over a century in Great Britain, this venerable seed firm crossed the Atlantic to set up operations here in the 1970s. While the selection of flowering plants probably cannot be matched, seed supplies are often limited. If you have your heart set on something new and unusual, send your order in early.

NONPROFIT SEED SOURCES

The following is a selected list of nonprofit organizations offering mail order seed programs. In each case you must be a member of the organization in order to participate. For many, these seed programs are the only way to obtain rare and unusual plants. For membership information send a self-addressed stamped envelope to the organization of your choice.

AMERICAN HORTICULTURAL SOCIETY
7931 East Boulevard Drive
Alexandria, Virginia 22308

AMERICAN ROCK GARDEN SOCIETY
Secretary, ARGS
P.O. Box 67
Millwood, New York 10546

BOWMAN'S HILL WILDFLOWER PRESERVE
Washington Crossing Historic Park
P.O. Box 103
Washington Crossing, Pennsylvania
 18977

GARDEN IN THE WOODS
New England Wild Flower Society
180 Hemenway Road
Framingham, Massachusetts
01701–2699

CORE LIST OF PLANT NURSERIES

Using the following seven nurseries, you should be able to obtain approximately 95 percent of the shrubs, groundcovers, and perennials described in this book.

BLUESTONE PERENNIALS
7211 Middle Ridge Road
Madison, Ohio 44057
(800) 852–5243

This is the best mail order bargain in the country. Bluestone offers the lowest prices and a quality of product and service that is among the highest in the business. In addition to a good, ever-expanding list of perennials, Bluestone offers a select list of shrubs.

CROWNSVILLE NURSERY
P.O. Box 797
Crownsville, Maryland 21032
(410) 923–2212
Catalogue: $2.00

This nursery specializes in beautiful but generally unrecognized flowers, many of them natives. There are also over 100 varieties of hostas featured in the catalogue, as well as an extensive daylily list. No other nursery can match the care it takes in packaging and shipping plants.

FORESTFARM
990 Tetherow Road
Williams, Oregon 97544–9599
(503) 846–6963
Catalogue: $3.00

Few firms can beat the extent of this nursery's shrub offerings. The selection is the largest I have come across; be aware, however, that the offerings do vary from year to year. If you can't find a plant listed, call. If they can obtain the seed, owners Ray and Peg Prag just may include it in their next catalogue. Forestfarm also offers many unusual perennials not found elsewhere.

HOLBROOK FARM & NURSERY
115 Lance Road, P.O. Box 368
Fletcher, North Carolina 28732
(704) 891–7790

Holbrook is at the top of the list in personal service and also offers an informative catalogue that is a pleasure to read. Allen W. Bush, the proprietor, frequently travels to Europe in search of new and interesting plants to offer. When at home in Fletcher, he personally answers all calls between 5 and 6 P.M. to help customers with their garden questions.

NATIVE GARDENS
5737 Fisher Lane
Greenback, Tennessee 37742
(615) 856–3350
Catalogue: $1.00

Meredith Bradford-Clebsch and Ed Clebsch own and operate this small nursery, which specializes in propagated wildflowers and a few woody plants. "Because we are most familiar with eastern species," they write, "they are our primary focus." Seeds are available for many of the plants offered.

THE PRIMROSE PATH
R.D. 2, Box 110
Scottdale, Pennsylvania 15683
(412) 887–6756

Catalogue: $2.00

This nursery offers a constantly changing selection of perennials, woodland plants, and alpines, many of them native species that are rarely offered. In recent years, owners Charles and Martha Oliver have been busy breeding their own beautiful plants—particularly in the heuchera, phlox, primula, and tiarella genera.

WHITE FLOWER FARM
Litchfield, Connecticut 06759–0050
(203) 496–9600

A granddaddy in the nursery mail order business, this company has done much to educate the American public on the beauty of perennials. The color pictures and information in the catalogue excel that found in many garden books. And large as it has grown, the firm still searches for—and finds—plants that are rarely offered by others.

SUPPLEMENTAL LIST
OF PLANT NURSERIES

BERKSHIRE FLOWER FARM
RFD 2, Box 380A
Shelburne Falls, Massachusetts 01370
   Owner Andrew E. Smith primarily sells his field-grown plants to garden centers and nurseries within driving distance of his hardy herbaceous plant business. He has a limited supply of cuckoo flowers (*Cardamine pratensis* 'Flore Pleno') and will sell these plants to individual gardeners through the mail. For further information, send a self-addressed stamped envelope to Mr. Smith at the above address.

MONTROSE NURSERY
P.O. Box 957
Hillsborough, North Carolina 27278
(919) 732–7787
Catalogue: $2.00
   This small nursery started in 1984 with the primary purpose of producing from seed and making available all cyclamen species. It has since expanded its interests and now offers a wide range of unusual perennials as well.

ONION MAN
30 Mt. Lebanon Street
Pepperell, Massachusetts 01463
Catalogue: Send self-addressed stamped
            envelope with three first-class
            stamps
   This business is literally a labor of love. Proprietor Mark McDonough is an architect by day and an allium aficionado at all other times.

In addition to publishing a quarterly newsletter called *G.A.R.L.I.C.*, he has also begun to offer mail order plants so that more gardeners will be able to enjoy the ease of care and the beauty of the allium genus. If he doesn't offer a particular allium, he is happy to refer gardeners to someone else who does.

WAYSIDE GARDENS
1 Garden Lane
Hodges, South Carolina 29695–0001
(800) 845–1124
   The service of this company is rarely surpassed—as is also true of its prices. It is famous for its sumptuously illustrated catalogues. Connoisseurs of plants, particularly shrubs, also know that Wayside offers many rare plants and superior specimens.

THE WILDWOOD FLOWER
Route 3, Box 165
Pittsboro, North Carolina 27312
Catalogue: Send self-addressed stamped
            envelope
   Several years ago, as a hobby, Thurman Maness decided to breed lobelias. The results were beautiful, sturdy plants. Gardeners soon beat a path to his door and The Wildwood Flower came into existence. In recent years he has broadened his offerings to include several little known plants that are perfect for shade gardens.

WINTERTHUR GARDEN
Winterthur, Delaware 19735
(800) 767–0500
   Through its Gift and Garden Sampler catalogue, Winterthur offers many of the beautiful and unusual plants grown on its grounds.

RECOMMENDED READING

GARDEN BOOKS

The following 10 books should answer any questions you have about selecting, growing, or designing with shade plants.

Classic Shade Gardening Books Though Morse wrote her book as an East Coast gardener and Schenk as a West Coast plantsman, both have much to teach shade gardeners across the country.

1 *Gardening in the Shade* by Harriet K. Morse (Timber Press, 242 pp.). Originally published in 1939 and then revised in 1962, this is a beautifully written book. Morse was way ahead of her time in championing the use of native plants.

2 *The Complete Shade Gardener* by George Schenk (Houghton Mifflin Company, 311 pp.). Schenk is my kind of writer—knowledgeable, witty, and great fun to read. Indeed, this book is so well written that even many a nongardener would enjoy the prose.

General Plant Books Using these books in combination, you will obtain all the information you need to grow a wide variety of plants.

1 *The National Arboretum Book of Outstanding Garden Plants* by Jacqueline Heriteau with Dr. H. Marc Cathey and the staff and consultants of the U.S. National Arboretum (Simon & Schuster, 293 pp.). Over 1,700 plants—including flowers, herbs, trees, shrubs, vines, and ornamental grasses—are described in this book. All were chosen for their "enduring beauty and resistance to pests and diseases." The large number of color photographs—over 450—make this an especially valuable reference source.

2 *Wyman's Gardening Encyclopedia* by Donald Wyman (Macmillan, 1221 pp.). Accurately billed as the most complete, authoritative one-volume gardening reference book on the market today, this encyclopedia gives both general gardening advice and detailed plant descriptions. Over 9,500 plants are listed.

Specific plant or plant category books. If you're interested in one particular group of plants, such as shrubs, the following are useful reference sources.

1. Shrubs

100 Great Garden Plants by William H. Frederick, Jr. (Timber Press, 216 pp.). Shrubs constitute over half the plants chosen for this book. The author, a professional landscape architect and ardent gardener, writes from personal experience in discussing how to grow and use all the plants. The interesting, informative text and numerous color photographs provide excellent guidelines on how to incorporate shrubs into the design of a garden.

2. Bulbs

Flowering Bulbs Indoors and Out by Theodore James, Jr., with photography by Harry Haralambou (Macmillan, 150 pp.). Illustrated with beautiful color photographs, this book is also packed with extremely useful information including whether or not a bulb is rodent proof, the kind of soil each bulb requires, the recommended planting depth, and any special maintenance needs.

3. Hostas

Each of the following provides useful information on the Hosta genus.

Hosta by Diana Grenfell (Timber Press, 208 pp.). A comprehensive study of hostas, this book presents an excellent discussion on the history of the genus in gardens as well as detailed descriptions of various species and cultivars, including uses, cultivation, and propagation.

The Hosta Book, edited and compiled by Paul Aden (Timber Press, 133 pp.). Noted Hosta breeder Paul Aden has written six chapters of this book and received contributions from eight other prominent gardeners. This has more color photographs than Grenfell's book.

4. Perennials

The two following titles are referred to throughout the text of this book. They are both wonderful information resources. Passionate gardeners, the authors cover considerably more than their subject areas. Armitage includes informative discussions on bulbs as well as herbaceous perennials. Clausen and Ekstrom's book covers many plants considered annuals in most parts of the country. Groundcovers, vines, and biennials are described in both books.

Herbaceous Perennial Plants by Allan M. Armitage (Varsity Press, 646 pp.). Opinionated and filled with interesting tidbits and historical lore, this book is written by a horticulture professor at the University of Georgia.

Armitage knows (and tells) from dirty-hand experience which plants will suffer in northern cold and which will wilt in southern humidity. A particularly useful feature is Armitage's inclusion of "Additional Reading" recommendations (an idea shamelessly copied here).

Perennials for American Gardens by Ruth Rogers Clausen and Nicolas H. Ekstrom (Random House, 633 pp.). Since this book covers many more plants than Armitage's (over 3,000 species) and is filled with hundreds of beautiful color photographs, there is not much room for personal opinion and historical information. Nevertheless, the authors cannot resist interjecting an occasional design suggestion or a plea for wider recognition of a plant's worthiness. This is the only book I have found that indicates whether or not a plant will tolerate humid conditions.

GARDEN MAGAZINES

I am an avid reader of all five magazines described below. They not only tell me of new developments in the world of gardening but introduce me to gardeners and gardens across the country.

Horticultural Society Publications. The following two are published bimonthly by nonprofit corporations and are part of membership benefits. *Green Scene* is also available on a subscription-only basis.

1. *American Horticulturist*
   7931 East Boulevard Drive
   Alexandria, Virginia 22308
   A publication of the American Horticultural Society, *American Horticulturist* covers gardening topics that illustrate the Society's goal of seeking to promote and recognize excellence in horticulture across America. There are superb in-depth profiles of plant genera as well as wonderful stories of the challenges of gardening in different areas of the country.

2. *Green Scene*
   The Pennsylvania Horticultural Society
   325 Walnut Street
   Philadelphia, Pennsylvania 19106
   With just two assistants, editor Jean Byrne does a great job in presenting richly illustrated articles on all aspects of gardening within the territory reached by her magazine's readership. The official publication of The Pennsylvania Horticultural Society, *Green Scene* subscriptions are now part of the membership benefits for groups as far away as Rhode Island, Ohio, and North Carolina.

Commercial Publications The following magazines are available at libraries and newsstands, as well as through yearly subscriptions.

1. *Fine Gardening*
   The Taunton Press, Inc.
   Newtown, Connecticut 06470–5506
   This nationwide magazine is essentially a reader-written publication. It is published bimonthly and features extensive first-person narratives of gardens and how they were created. Other gardeners write descriptions of their favorite plant species or genera as well as how they construct fences, create composting piles, etc.

2. *Flower & Garden*
   KC Publishing, Inc.
   700 West 47th Street
   Suite 310
   Kansas City, Missouri 64112
   This bimonthly magazine has the broadest circulation, reaching over 600,000 home gardeners across the country. Recently it has begun to champion a concern for the environment by showing how gardeners can contribute not only to a healthier but also a more beautiful planet in a responsible manner.

3. *Horticulture*
   Horticulture Limited Partnership
   98 North Washington Street
   Boston, Massachusetts 02114
   Despite its subtitle, "The Magazine of American Gardening," this has a strong international slant. It is the most frequently published garden magazine, with 10 issues a year. There is an emphasis on design, and stunning garden photographs; indeed, there are often photographic essays with little or no text.